GOD MOMENTS

UNEXPECTED ENCOUNTERS
IN THE ORDINARY

"Andy Otto brilliantly and simply helps all of us discover a God who wants to relate to us in the ordinary messiness of our day-to-day lives. Easily accessible yet profound and inspiring, this book is a modern-day spiritual treasure."

Rev. Dave Dwyer, C.S.P.
Director of *Busted Halo*

"I'm an avid reader of Andy Otto's blogging observations about the spiritual life. Finally, we have a book that focuses on a theme close to the heart of his writing: a God who is found in all things. Andy draws us to look lovingly at a God who is always already looking lovingly at us. *God Moments* is a book for those who are unsure about how to discover God but might find themselves drawn like a magnet to Christian faith."

Tim Muldoon
Catholic theologian at Boston College and
coauthor of *The Discerning Parent*

"*God Moments* is inviting and inspiring. Whether Andy Otto is invoking *It's a Wonderful Life* while reflecting on the power of Ignatian prayer or sharing stories from his own journey of discernment, he takes the spiritual and makes it practical. This engaging book will help you recognize God in all things and use that knowledge to become the person you were created to be."

Ginny Kubitz Moyer
Author of *Mary and Me* and *Random MOMents of Grace*

"In an earnest and accessible way, Andy Otto gives us a trademark, joy-filled take on Ignatian spirituality. *God Moments* is equally compelling and nourishing to any reader seeking a closer relationship with God."

Matt Weber
CatholicTV host and author of *Operating on Faith*

GOD MOMENTS

UNEXPECTED ENCOUNTERS
IN THE ORDINARY

ANDY OTTO

Ave Maria Press AVE Notre Dame, Indiana

Founded in 1865, Ave Maria Press is a ministry of the United States Province of Holy Cross.

www.avemariapress.com

Paperback: ISBN-13 978-1-59471-647-8

E-book: ISBN-13 978-1-59471-648-5

Cover image © iStockphoto.com.

Cover and text design by Katherine J. Ross.

Printed and bound in the United States of America.

Library of Congress Cataloging-in-Publication Data is available.

For Sarah and Eva

CONTENTS

INTRODUCTION

Consider where you are right now, this place you've been given as shelter, the breakfast you had this morning. Notice your breath, the blinking of your eyes, your ability to read this. Consider the brain power you have, which has given you reason to make decisions that have lead you up to this moment in your life. As you opened this book or turned the page, did you notice the miracle of your fingers and the tiny muscle movements that made it happen? Consider the hundreds of processes going on inside of you right now. Whom do you most care about? What are you good at? What are your talents?

God has given this all to you. God sustains all of this in existence. God is the life-giving Source. This truth enriches our seemingly mundane actions with a greater awareness of the goodness within them. This is finding God in all things.

In Ronald Rolheiser's masterpiece *The Holy Longing*, he introduces the idea of a "God with skin." It's rooted in the Incarnation of Christ, where God took on literal flesh—skin—and walked the earth. The Incarnation is the foundation of Ignatian spirituality. There we find a God who is concrete and whom we can experience. Rolheiser says, "The God of the incarnation has real flesh on earth and speaks to us in the bread and butter of our lives, through things that have skin—historical circumstance, our families, our neighbors, our churches, and that borderline-psychotic friend who painfully reminds us that we are not God."[1]

The Incarnation of God is not just about God's coming to earth in the person of Jesus but about Christ's continued presence and "fleshiness" in the world. My hope is to take this idea further and make it practical for our everyday living. Through just a few short years, I discovered how the God with skin appears at practically every waking moment.

Living a deeply spiritual life is not just about morals or obligations. It's about something deeper, which our churches—at times—fail to tap into. Much of my spiritual growth has occurred in the normal places of daily life: at school, at work, in the car, or with friends. My spirituality is heavily influenced by Ignatian spirituality, the most important principle of which is finding God in all things, in these plain and ordinary spaces, and within ourselves. God's presence dwells in everything. God gives life and being and existence to everything, so finding God in all things is just a matter of paying attention. You look at spring buds on the trees, and you see God giving them life. You feel the warmth of the sun on your face, and you sense God comforting you. A stranger smiles at you, and suddenly you feel connected to all of God's family. In the hustle of life, it's easy for us to miss these God moments. Time and time again, we must remind ourselves to look and listen more attentively to the ways God is present to us.

I first learned about finding God in all things with the story of St. Ignatius of Loyola, who founded the Jesuit order (which I was a part of for a short time). Ignatius was born into wealth around the turn of the sixteenth century in northern Spain. As a Castilian military governor, he fought for his people—a literal knight in shining armor. Caught up with his nobility and fancy new castle, he dreamed of living the good life and indulged in gambling, dueling, and having affairs. Then, when he was fighting the French in battle, his castle was stormed and a cannonball shattered his leg. As he recovered in bed, he continued dreaming of a fantastic life, but how that would play out would not be in the way he expected.

During his recuperation, he read about the lives of Christ and the saints and chose instead to live fighting for God. The benefit of all this time in recovery was that he had time to pay attention to his feelings. As he weighed his desires for a life of knighthood with his desires for more saintly living, he discovered that his feelings pointed him to a life of following God rather than seeking riches and status. This was the beginning of Ignatian spirituality. Through his life experiences, travels, and encounters, he came to notice a God with skin who was communicating with him through those experiences and people.

After I learned this story, I began to understand, like St. Ignatius, how God takes on flesh in the various experiences and people around me. The "all things" in which we desire to find God includes you and me. We not only encounter God in the world but, like St. Ignatius, *we* give God skin. "All things" really means that God is not limited to any one thing or any one person in particular. A church does not contain God *more* than a field of corn. A priest is not more holy than a single mother. God is uncontained and unconfined.

———

When I met my wife-to-be, we realized we had a shared spirituality. And when it came time to enter into the sacrament of Marriage, we wanted to be intentional about it, so we asked ourselves why we were getting married. What was the purpose of forming a lifelong partnership with each other? Our answer was not just about how much we loved each other or how we wanted to grow old together. Our answer was that we wanted *to change the world*.

As people of faith, we wanted our marriage to affect the world in a positive way. We wanted the sacrament of our Marriage to be a way in which God broke into the world. When people looked at the fruits of our love and actions, we wanted them to see God manifested through us. We simply wanted to live our Christian call of loving God and neighbor and concretely bring God's love to others. And we could do that better together than on our own.

St. Paul says, "I have become all things to all people, that I might by all means save some" (1 Cor 9:22b, NRSV). He alludes to the need for us, as people of God who serve and love and minister to others, to be adaptable enough so that we may be able compassionately to companion others. This means that we can be present for the single mother as much as for the widowed man. We can be God's loving presence as much for a starving orphan as we can for a coworker. God's limits know no bounds, which means that God's reach manifests itself in us in a multitude of ways.

St. Paul expands on how we can be all things to all people: "There are different kinds of spiritual gifts, but the same Spirit gives them. There are different ways of serving, but the same Lord is served. There are different abilities to perform service, but the same God gives ability to all for their particular service. The Spirit's presence is shown in some way in each person for the good of all" (1 Cor 12:4–7, GNT). The mission is the same: to serve God and serve our neighbor. But each of us carries it out in different ways and with different gifts. In this way, that last verse can be fulfilled: "The Spirit's presence is shown in some way in each person for the good of all."

Day-to-day living reveals how God uses us in different ways. One day my conversation with a coworker turned into her pouring out her heart to me about her past struggles. This was a God moment for me, so I sat and listened lovingly. As a high school teacher, I often feel God using me to empathize with my students' struggles of growing up. There have been other times I've sat with the dying and have been a loving presence for them. Each circumstance is very different and requires us to adapt, but each circumstance shows the same thing: that God can be found in us, that "all things" simply means letting God be present through us for whatever person or situation presents itself.

—

I've discovered the God with skin can be found through *awareness* and *prayer* and that we give God skin through *discernment* and *decision-making*. These two themes are the foundation for this book. This book is less about me and more about you. While I will offer personal anecdotes from time to time, the hope is that *God Moments* will draw you into a deeper awareness of God's concrete presence in your life as I share ways in which I've become more aware of the divine presence in my own life. Whether or not you have heard of Ignatian spirituality before, this book will serve as a practical companion as you explore the ways that God appears before you in an ordinary and messy world.

Ignatius says that we should always let the Spirit of God lead. While God may use the following pages and chapters to speak to you, you cannot confine the God with skin even to this book. You may discover that the fruits and "aha" moments you get within these pages will unfold more once you've put this book down.

Just days after leaving the Jesuits, I began GodInAllThings. com, a blog and website devoted to Ignatian spirituality. It was the fruit of what God had shown me in the past years, and it has unfolded now into this book. I encourage you to use this book and the website as resources. But don't make books and websites your only resources. God has created a stunning world outside your door to explore, and God has also given you the gift of prayer. You'll often find that more comes from *within* than from any book or blog. Let this book just be the spark at the beginning of a long and slow burn of an encounter with the God with skin.

1

AWARENESS

I grew up in a fairly typical Catholic family that went to church weekly, prayed at meals and before bed, and was involved in religious classes. Like many "cradle Catholics," I blew through the sacraments without much thought. My mother gave me a list of my sins to take to my first Confession, I made my first Communion, and then I reached Confirmation. The teacher told us that Confirmation was the point when we could make an adult decision to continue as Catholics, that it was *our* choice, not our parents'. This was a minor turning point for me. While many of my classmates stopped going to church after Confirmation, I maintained an interest. Yet for me, prayer was about praying to a distant God who mysteriously chose whether or not to answer my prayers. It was a fairly uninvolved God in my mind: a God who appeared as static, dusty crucifixes, religious statues, and formulaic prayers. My favorite part of going to my family's church was the donuts after Mass. My undergraduate years didn't do much for my faith. I continued to attend church out of obligation, and I didn't really pray all that much.

After graduating, I began working in Boston and decided to join an online dating site. I didn't know exactly why it was important to me, but I set my preferences to only return matches from Christian women. I soon began dating a Protestant girl who was alive in her faith. She invited me to her weekly Bible study and introduced me to her friends, who were also on fire with a love for God. What struck me in our faith sharing was how much these women and men, who worked in all sorts of fields, could find God in their everyday lives. My life was so routine, and I hadn't yet moved beyond going to church out of obligation. Church seemed like something I had to do, like flossing or going to work, in order to get my "spiritual paycheck"—whatever that was good for. God still seemed one-dimensional and uninvolved. How was it that these people at the Bible study had such intimate encounters with God?

I began reading more, learning about my faith, attending a young-adult group at my church, and meeting with a Jesuit spiritual director. I had heard about Ignatian spirituality at church and through my brother, who was a Jesuit studying for priesthood. My spiritual director helped me discover, for the first time, how to find God in all things—the heart of Ignatian spirituality. He helped me pray using my imagination, and my awareness opened to the ways that God was touching me in my daily life. God took on skin by appearing all around me: in the people on my commuter bus, in the sun shining off the snow, in my girlfriend making me a meal. I could finally see how beauty was a sign of God's presence and how others were *bringing God to me* through their love and friendship. I could not believe how my relationship with God was beginning to grow and how prayer for me was becoming more than asking God for things.

Prayer became something I lived and breathed. Prayer was not just folding my hands and speaking to God but *awareness*, moments of gazing at the faces of people sharing the bus on my commute or watching my dog pounce through the snow during her first winter. It was if God leapt from out of the clouds down to my earthly reality and became intimately involved in my life. God was no longer just located in church on Sunday or in Bible passages discussed in religious-education classes. It was like the joy of Christmas morning when you realize that Christ's birth was not just some sanitized fairy tale but God's radical leap from heaven to earth, becoming human so he could be intimately involved in our lives.

At times prayer for me became a conversation with God, but I also had quiet nights in prayer when there was no light in my bedroom but a small tealight candle in a red glass votive cup. It was simple and disarming. My prayer had no words. It was nothing more than watching the flicker of the flame and feeling God's presence in the room. There was something about the flame that revealed God to me. A flame has a life of its own, flickering and moving on its own, even without an apparent breeze. Sometimes the orange-red flame goes wild, while at other moments it sits calmly and still. It was alive like me, like the Spirit, and was providing warmth and light as if by magic. But the force behind it was God.

This is the simple magic we see in a sunset or an ant crawling across the floor. They are the simple things of beauty that are outside our control yet have amazing lives of their own. I'll never forget an evening of Taizé prayer I attended when the thin taper candle I was holding in my fist started moving on a rhythm. It was my pulse—the blood coursing through my arteries and veins—that was causing the taper to move, pulse by pulse. I remember staring at it, knowing that it was not I consciously moving it but the blood that God was causing to pulse rhythmically through my hand.

Now the simple act of lighting a candle becomes a prayer for me, initiating that flame which I've come to see as so close to God's essence, providing me light and comfort. And I suppose that magic, as I call it, is that life force beyond me—God sustaining and causing, creating beauty through a flickering flame and the pulse of my blood. These things can be explained through physics and biology, but there is something there still hidden, which is why I can see God there.

C. S. Lewis uses the word *magic* in his book *Letters to Malcom: Chiefly on Prayer*: "I should define magic in this sense as 'objective efficacy which cannot be further analysed.' . . . Now the value, for me, of the magical element of Christianity is this. It is a permanent witness that the heavenly realm, certainly no less than the natural universe and perhaps very much more, is a realm of objective facts. . . . One cannot conceive a more completely 'given,' or, if you like, a more 'magical,' fact than the existence of God as causa sui."[1]

Deep stuff. In essence, the "magic" of the universe, of the flame, the pulse, the sunset, and the ant is a witness to the existence of God. But the magical element cannot be gotten rid of by mere explanation. I think that even though I can explain the photons and energy of the flame in my votive cup and I can explain how the impulses from my heart caused the pressure of my blood to move the taper in my hand, there remains a wonder and awe that has its source in God. And that invisible Source becomes visible in the material world. God creates those physical and bodily processes that make my hand pulse.

Michael Gungor's song "Cannot Keep You" speaks about our boxing in of God, our trying to confine God to churches, rituals, or scripture.

> So we will find you in the streets
> And we will find you in the prisons
> And even in our Bibles and churches.[2]

When we confine God *only* to the faith of our childhood or rules and doctrine, we make God very small. The God with skin is a deeply personal God, intimately involved in the nooks and crannies of our lives. This God is ready to appear not just in church but in a listening friend, in a remarkable teacher, in a gorgeous sunset, on the street, and even in us.

As time went on, God became part of my everyday life. Through the influence of my Jesuit spiritual director and my exposure to others in the Jesuit world, I fell in love with Ignatian spirituality. Imbued with my newly discovered spirituality, I began to see religious life and priesthood as a way I could live out my life.

It happened almost all of a sudden one evening. As I was winding down for the night after a long day at work, I was online searching for stuff on Ignatian spirituality and came across a Jesuit vocation page that listed steps for discerning a religious vocation. As I read through each step, I realized that it was describing exactly what I was experiencing. I felt pangs in my body as if God was trying literally to take hold of my heart. I broke down weeping. *What was God trying to say to me?*

The feeling of being called to something more was a very physical experience for me. God was trying to communicate with me so intentionally that I *felt* it. It's a feeling you may have experienced when you fell in love or felt a tug of the heartstrings in a time of sorrow. These are the specific moments worth paying attention to, moments when God takes on a "fleshiness" within us.

I set up an emergency meeting with my spiritual director, and over the next year I discerned to enter the Jesuits. The discernment process itself was a profound encounter with the God with skin. And as I'll mention later, making prayerful decisions in our lives is one of the primary ways *we* give God skin.

For two and a half years in the Jesuits, I had the chance to minister in a multitude of ways. For several weeks in Jamaica, I could see God in the deep devotion of a people struggling in poverty, who every Sunday donned their one set of nice clothes and worshiped at church, praising God for their many blessings. What did I thank God for when I went to church solely out of obligation? These people had so little and I was so privileged, yet they had such gratitude for God's goodness!

I also had the opportunity to sit with the sick as a hospital chaplain and feed and bathe the dying in hospice. Many were grateful for my presence, sharing personal life stories with me, even life regrets—with me, a stranger. But as a chaplain, I represented God to them, a safe confidant who somehow made God present to them. My patients taught me a lot, too—many showing great faith and love for life despite having terminal illnesses. I would often sigh in my reflection during these times, both humbled by being used by God for others and feeling inadequate in my own faith after meeting strangers with amazing conviction and love of God.

As a Jesuit, I also made the Spiritual Exercises, a thirty-day silent retreat created by St. Ignatius. During that month, through prayer and scripture, I got to encounter Jesus Christ in a way that I never had before. My time as a Jesuit let me encounter the incarnate God in countless people and circumstances. I'll mention more about this in the chapter on discernment, but what I learned about God and discernment as a Jesuit was critical in my decision to leave religious life and pursue marriage and a theology degree.

———

An intimate relationship with God and a fruitful spiritual life require a *real* encounter with God. My first raw, fall-off-the-horse encounter with God was that tearful evening when I felt called to religious life. God was revealed on the Jesuit vocation site, in the pangs in my heart, and in my tears—what Ronald Rolheiser calls the "bread and butter" of our lives, those things we can touch and see and feel. Most may not have a profound conversion experience, yet God still appears in the "fleshy" and *ordinary* parts of life.

When we read the Bible, we can take for granted how often God appeared to humanity. Theology would call such signs of God's presence *theophanies*. Moses experienced this when God appeared to him through the burning bush. Abraham did so as well, encountering God when an angel of the Lord appeared to him. Our day-to-day living might not involve such extraordinary encounters with God like Moses and Abraham experienced, but our encounters with the divine will occur as we go about our day. Each and every day God appears to us in ways so plain and ordinary that we often miss them.

A sixth grader I taught once asked me, "How come God doesn't speak to us anymore like he did to those in the Bible?" "God does speak to us!" I responded. "God speaks to us every day through prayer, our feelings, and our experiences." Often it is only after we reflect back on our day, looking for signs of God, that those daily theophanies become more noticeable. You realize that your friend whom you were lamenting to was God listening to you. You discover that a beam of sunlight that poked through the clouds and warmed your face was God comforting you. This is the incarnate God reaching out to us in the ordinary.

What does *ordinary* mean exactly? When I see icons and paintings of Christ or the saints, I see much piety and holiness. The subject of the picture usually has some sort of halo or glow about him or her and may be looking up to heaven. Images of Christ often show him on the clouds surrounded by angels, who are ministering to him. This is not the kind of thing I'm talking about. Seeing God in the ordinary means recognizing that God came down to earth!

A while back, I traveled to Portland, Maine, for a weekend with my wife, Sarah, and as we walked past a Catholic church, we looked over and saw a side door open to reveal a priest dressed in his clerics. But what the father had in his grasp was a bag of trash he was taking out. "There he is," Sarah joked. "There's Father."

What a great image, we thought. We didn't see it as some strange metaphor, but just that: the parish priest taking out the trash. It was a great image because, in an age when we figuratively place priests into a box or on a pedestal—they have to be this way or that—it is important to see that they, like us, have to do chores and domestic work and pay bills. Priests are human. They're ordinary. But for some reason we fashion an image of them like Bing Crosby's character Fr. O'Malley in *The Bells of St. Mary's*.

When I was in religious life, I had a taste of that. Others I served saw me as someone picture-perfect. They watched their language in front of me (God forbid they offend a priest-to-be!). They always asked me to say grace (somehow my prayers were more effective than the next person's). They assumed I was probably sinless, that I had my life together and all figured out, that I had the answers, and that I always practiced what I preached. What they didn't see was the side of me that sometimes reacted negatively toward my brothers in community. They didn't know that my superior once called me selfish. They didn't know about my doubts in my vocation, that I had feelings for someone—I didn't have it all figured out. They didn't know my weaknesses. And just like them, I had to take out the trash.

I think our images of Jesus can often tend to be overly polished, too. Jesus, even though he was God incarnate, also probably had to take out the trash. His human life had its own hardships, chores, relationship challenges, and weaknesses. Even though Jesus was divine, he was fully human. As St. Paul said, "Though he was in the form of God, [Jesus] did not regard equality with God as something to be exploited, but emptied himself, taking the form of a slave, being born in human likeness" (Phil 2:6–7, NRSV). The priest taking out the trash at that church in Portland reminded me that everyday, mundane labors were places where the divine can show up in the ordinary.

I'm always fascinated by how easily children can see the presence of God in the most mundane things. I was once teaching a lesson to sixth graders on how feelings are important to understanding God and ourselves. I asked the children to think about the best moment they experienced yesterday, and one girl shared that she had been to a trampoline park. "How did you feel when you went there?" I asked. She said she felt overjoyed and happy. "And what can that feeling of joy and happiness tell you about

God?" I asked. One student responded, "It tells you God loves you." Yes! Something as simple as an activity of fun that gives you joy can indicate God's love. And even when the feeling is more negative, we can learn that God is still present with us.

St. Paul writes, "Ever since God created the world, his invisible qualities, both his eternal power and his divine nature, have been clearly seen; they are perceived in the things that God has made" (Rom 1:20a, GNT). We often recognize God's goodness when we're awestruck by the beauty of the created world. Beauty is something that is actually very ordinary. We encounter it every day. Holly Bird writes, "Beauty engages our senses. It appeals to our nature as embodied beings. Simone Weil writes of beauty as an 'incarnation' of the divine in our world, like the sacraments. Just as the Word became flesh to bring God's salvation to the world, God communicates grace with us through sensory experiences. Beauty is one medium by which God communicates with humanity."[3]

To consider beauty as a medium of communication may seem profound, but it is nothing new. For as long as time itself humans have been using art as a form of communication. Whether through cave paintings or stirring musical compositions, beauty transmits something of the truth of God. Have you ever seen a stunning painting that stopped you in your tracks or caused your jaw to hang open in awe? Have you ever heard a song that touched your very core and brought you outside of yourself? The haunting theme from the film *The Mission* always does it for me. It makes me feel as if my life is part of a bigger purpose. Moments such as these are important to our understanding of God. If you pass by beautiful art too quickly, you'll mistake it for just the result of a human creation.

While we may find God in the concrete "stuff" of the universe, there's a natural tendency to look beyond to those unseen realities of God. Saints are pictured piously looking up to heaven, yearning for their "true home." Looking into the invisible realities of God is fine. But we can fall into the danger of placing God solely in the transcendent realm, where this world becomes less of a home and more of a waiting room. As a result, we paint pictures of angels and heaven and forget how God created every atom of matter in our present home and that it too is holy. As the Nicene Creed says, "I believe in one God, the Father almighty, maker of heaven and earth, of all things visible and invisible."

Just days after Pope Francis was elected, he celebrated Holy Thursday Mass not from the Basilica of St. John Lateran, his church, but instead at a prison. I, like many, was surprised. Some were disappointed and expected the pope to continue a custom that employed high liturgy and opulence. They claimed that the grandiosity and intricate artwork of the Basilica revealed a more transcendent God than did a prison.

We must be careful of certain spiritual practices that simply become an escape from everyday ordinariness. In the desire to see something transcendent that "points" to God's glory, we forget that God's glory is pointing to the ordinary and the plain! We cannot box God into just a few "holy" places. Richard Rohr says that true Christian mysticism does not distinguish between the sacred and profane. "The whole universe and all events are sacred (doorways to the divine) for those who know how to see."[4] By washing the feet of prisoners at Holy Thursday Mass, Pope Francis found God in the ordinary. He saw God's presence in what otherwise might be considered "profane" or "unholy." If we truly believe God is in all things then we can find God not only in high liturgy and transcendent-looking cathedrals but also in a coffee-table Mass in someone's home and even in the dirty feet of a prisoner.

God is in the "dirt" of the here and now. That is the sacramental life of Catholics. Stuff like bread and wine, fire and water, oil and palm leaves do not just point to God. The beauty of these things shows us that God's presence enters into those things, making them holy. When God became incarnate in Jesus, he gave humanity itself a new holiness. He sanctified the "earthly" things of this world. Jesus spoke often about his kingdom and what was beyond our world, but he most certainly showed people the holiness of the ordinary. "Look at the birds of the air and the lilies of the field!" he exclaimed. God cares for those things as intimately as he cares for us. Jesus used mud from the earth to restore sight to a blind person. The earth and the divine are interconnected.

Each year I look forward to the Easter Vigil. Before I came to understand how God's presence could be found in the ordinary, I saw the Easter Vigil as just a very long Mass. But the service is the high point of the Catholic liturgical year. It employs Catholic sacramentality in full force. The service begins in darkness, where a fire is lighted and blessed. Then the light increases as congregants pass the flame, candle to candle, filling the church with flickering light. The scriptures are then broken open, telling the story of God's involvement throughout history. The Jesuit parish I attended in Boston even had dancers, giving movement to the Word proclaimed. Then new members come into the church through the water of Baptism, they're confirmed with sacred oil and the laying on of hands, and then everyone receives Christ in the elements of bread and wine. The Easter Vigil became for me a sensual experience of God touching me through the seemingly ordinary elements of fire, word, water, oil, bread, wine, and even dance.

When we acknowledge God being present in all the ordinary things around us, we're not making things idols, as if a beautiful tree or sunset *is* God (this is called pantheism). Instead, we see that all things are *part* of God, who is beyond the created world (this is called pan*en*theism). St. John of Damascus once said, "I do not worship matter; I worship the Creator of matter who became matter for my sake, who willed to take His abode in matter; who worked out my salvation through matter."[5]

Finding God in all things begins in the matter of creation simply because *we are* the matter of creation. At this moment,

you and I are not in the heavenly realm. We are limited to our
human bodies, which need a certain amount of oxygen and food
to survive. We have to use our legs to get from place to place or
invent vehicles to take us to more distant locations. We're bound
by space and time.

I cannot go up to heaven to encounter God. I have to locate
God within the boundaries of the created world I'm in. Even
when we have a transcendent or spiritual experience of God, our
human senses are engaged. God uses our bodies—our feelings,
emotions, and senses—to communicate with us. The pangs of the
heart or the spiritual thoughts that arise may indeed come from
God, but they still reside within our human perception.

So we find God in the feet of prisoners, in our thoughts and
feelings, and in the people around us. Pope Francis's simplicity
and step back from pomp and circumstance does not disregard
the transcendent. It simply reminds us that God's transcendent
Spirit resides also in the forgotten and "dirty" parts of the world,
such as in the experiences of the marginalized, the oppressed,
and the poor, and in the plain and everyday circumstances of
ordinary people like you and me. Jesus' disciples, who were as
ordinary as can be, are examples of how God takes the dirt and
transforms it into life-giving soil.

Consider the symbol of the life-giving soil from which God
created the first human being. The name scripture gives to Adam
literally comes from the Hebrew word for soil. God breathes life
into Adam's lungs. Our God is a god who acts and creates with
the stuff of the earth. The scriptures talk about a farmer planting
seed: "He sleeps at night, is up and about during the day, and all
the while the seeds are sprouting and growing. Yet he does not
know how it happens" (Mk 4:27, GNT). St. Ignatius said that God
labors for us continually. That labor also happens on the molec-
ular level with things we cannot even see; it is God continuing
the action of creation.

In Acts 3, Peter is speaking to the Israelites, who were responsible for the death of Jesus. In his exhortation, we encounter the beautiful and terrible line, "The author of life you put to death" (Acts 3:15a, NABRE). It is beautiful because it acknowledges that Jesus, as a human manifestation of God, authored, penned, and created life—indeed, he invented life itself! Yet it is terrible because we squashed the life from Life itself by putting Jesus to death. Ultimately, the sin of humanity did not succeed, and Jesus rose from the dead never to die again. It's a jarring reality: the One who authored life, we killed. But when Jesus came back from death, his love-filled action (creation), just as before, continued.

In Emmaus the disciples did not recognize Jesus when he told them about the scriptures, nor did they even recognize his face (see Lk 24:13–35, NRSV). No, they recognized him only once he broke the bread. Jesus was "made known to them" (v. 35) through a *concrete* action involving bread. They say actions speak louder than words, right? Here is our God, a human who eats and acts, using the matter of the world to reveal himself to us.

Two millennia ago, the most profound action of God was being born into this world in the person of Jesus. This is what we tend to think of as the Incarnation: Christmas, Jesus' thirty-three-year life, and so on. But in the Christian understanding, incarnation continued long past Jesus' time and is ongoing. "Sure, God is everywhere," you may respond. But, as Ronald Rolheiser says in his book *The Holy Longing*, "A God who is everywhere is just as easily nowhere."[6] We need a God who is touchable and physically real: a God with skin.

In the Gospel of Luke, we witness Jesus appearing to his friends (see Lk 24:36–43, NRSV). At first they're terrified and startled. They think he's a ghost. Jesus had told them before his death how the scriptures foretold his death and resurrection, but they had not seemed to listen. However, instead of giving them a slap to knock some sense into them and show them that he's real, he says, "Touch me and see" (v. 39). At this point, touching him is what it's going to take for the disciples to realize that Jesus is not a ghost but true flesh and bones. And as further proof, perhaps in a slight tongue-in-cheek move, he says, "Have you anything here to eat?" (v. 41).

Rolheiser says that we need a similar experience for ourselves: a God who is truly touchable. The Body of Christ is more than a metaphor for a group of Christian believers. You and I and our family and neighbors and friends are all *literally* part of Christ's body, one that you and I touch and interact with every day! Each believer, with his or her skin and bones, makes up the Body of Christ, as much as the Jesus who said to his disciples, "Touch me." Our God is more than just a distant, ghostly spirit.

I remember, when I was about five or six years old, asking my mother how a woman becomes pregnant with a baby. She told me that you have to "pray very hard." That night I prayed hard to God for a baby brother or sister. Needless to say, my mother was not pregnant the next morning. It seemed that God either didn't care to answer my prayer or had better things to do. In my childhood, I figured God was distant and mostly uninvolved.

In my childhood bedroom I had a shelf full of prayer cards, Bibles, and crosses as well as a Mass book and a beige plastic statue of Jesus. These for me pointed to that distant God. I suppose they made God a bit more visible to me as a child. I could pick up a book and read about God, pray a written prayer to God, or touch a statue of Jesus. Faith sometimes must come through believing in the invisible, but quite often it comes through touch and concrete things, like my childhood religious articles. But as my faith matured, I could touch God through creation and the palpable things of my life: my relationships, my experiences—the dirt of the here and now. God became less distant. The disciples, twenty centuries ago, got to touch Jesus' wounds. For us, it's the idea of finding God in all things and in all people that gives God skin: in a sunset, a newborn baby, a kiss, an embrace. It's the palpability found in the sacraments or in the bread and the wine at Mass.

The seven official sacraments of the Catholic Church, such as Baptism and the Eucharist, are sacred and privileged encounters with Christ that lead us toward salvation. Yet they are so basic, using ordinary elements from the earth: water, oil, wheat, and grapes. The "sacramental reality," on the other hand, takes the encounter with Christ we have in the official sacraments and broadens it to include the ordinary reality of everyday life. As Rolheiser writes, "God takes on flesh so that every home becomes a church, every child becomes the Christ-child, and all food and drink become a sacrament. God's many faces are now everywhere, in flesh, tempered and turned down, so that our human eyes can see him. God, in his many-faced face, has become as accessible, and visible, as the nearest water tap. That is the why of the incarnation."[7]

The early church fathers, such as Iranaeus and Athanasius, stated that God took on flesh so that, by our entering into relationship with Christ, we could share in his divinity—"so that we might become God."[8] The Incarnation of Christ and creation are deeply interconnected. The way we become God on this earth is by the very fact of our creation. Just like Jesus, you and I are made up of billions of cells and atoms; God placed each component there with great purpose. Our cells constantly regenerate and are replaced—this is creation at work. Psalm 139 uses the metaphor of being knit, revealing a Creator who cares deeply about incarnation. In "O God, You Search Me," Bernadette Farrell's musical adaptation of the psalm, is the line, "For the wonder of who I am, I praise you/Safe in your hands, all creation is made new."[9] What wonder indeed, knowing how God is made manifest in each one of us!

Knowing that I have a God with skin, incarnate in those around me, completely magnifies my appreciation of loved ones. When my wife listens to me, Christ is there listening. When my parents offer me a meal, Christ is there cooking. When a friend offers me a ride, Christ is there driving. Each action they take in *their* skin is a mini-incarnation, here and now, giving *God* skin. And each action I take in the Spirit of God also makes God incarnate to the world.

GOD'S GAZE

When I was a Jesuit, I worked as a hospital chaplain. I once suggested to one of my patients a unique kind of prayer. I told him to acknowledge his surroundings, his feelings at the moment, and his life situation. Then I said, "Imagine God gazing down upon you. What does God see? How does God feel?" He was struggling with a deep self-pity in his chronic medical condition. When I returned to his room the next day, he told me he prayed this way the entire day. I asked him about the experience, and with tears in his eyes he said to me, "I felt God looking upon me with love."

This loving gaze from God is the foundation of an Ignatian meditation often referred to as the "Meditation on the Incarnation." We imagine the three persons of the Trinity (God the Father, Jesus Christ, and the Holy Spirit) gazing upon the world and seeing all the chaos going on: the laughing and crying, the marrying and divorcing, the building and destroying, the loving and hating, the revolting and peacemaking, the birthing and dying, and so on. Then the Trinity decides, out of love, to send the second person of the Trinity to become human, redeem us, and remind humanity of God's love and healing. This is the moment at which God enters our world and takes on skin.

Much of my life has involved looking for God, trying to understand what God has wanted of me. When I was young, I searched too hard for God in formulaic prayer and in holy water, in church groups and in scripture. I became obsessed with the mysterious messages of the book of Revelation. A relative told me about the symbolism of the book and about the Second Coming of Christ on a white horse descending from the clouds, so I pestered my Confirmation teacher about this. She knew little about Revelation and was quite annoyed at my questions. Some of this seeking was helpful; some was not. I would sit in church with my family and look at Jesus' face on the crucifix, but I would never notice him looking back at me. Sometimes the most revelatory prayer is allowing God to look back at us. God sees us as we are and loves us with every rough edge and nick we have.

By allowing God to gaze upon him, my hospital patient could see through his own self-pity and realize that God sincerely loves him as he is. The Incarnation of Jesus Christ is proof of this loving gaze. This is precisely the point Ignatius was trying to make by including this meditation in his Spiritual Exercises. It's a prayer where we do no speaking. We do no searching. Instead, God's gaze does the speaking.

I often feel God's gaze upon me while driving. One evening after a busy day of classes, I was driving home. My normal tendency was either to put on NPR to catch up on the news or to play some upbeat music. After about forty-five minutes of driving, I was nearly home, but I noticed that I was still feeling the stress of the day. I wanted the last few minutes of my drive to be peaceful before I got home to my wife. Without much thought, I switched to the spa channel on the satellite radio. As the calming music began to play, I glanced outside toward the evening sky, and I could see a blurry moon looking down through the clouds. The moment seemed to touch my heart. As I gazed at the blurry orb in the night sky, I felt the comfort of God gazing upon me, loving me as I am, busy and stressed.

Driving west on the Massachusetts Turnpike often reminds me of my trip to the Jesuit novitiate the day before beginning a new chapter in my life. The changing colors of fall especially bring about memories of that transition period, which was both exciting and a bit frightening. But what I remember about that drive west was that God was with me, going with me to a new place, loving me no matter what lay ahead.

When we imagine God gazing at us, we are opened up to new ways of seeing ourselves and new ways of loving ourselves. My spiritual director once gave me a list of "feeling words" and suggested that I imagine God gazing on me as I reflected on my day or week. He told me to imagine what God might have been feeling and to use the list as a guide. When I got in an argument with a coworker, did God feel *aggravated* like I did? Did God share in my *heartbreak* when my friend canceled a date at the last minute? When I printed my last final paper for school, did God feel *elated* like I did? Perhaps God felt *touched* when I expressed my gratitude in prayer. Indeed, God is alongside of us in every ordinary moment, loving us.

Knowing God's loving gaze is essential to the spiritual life. When we see that God looks upon us lovingly and not as a harsh judge, there's a good chance a deeper relationship will form. We may even stop trying to be someone else and be the person God made us to be.

ORDINARY MIRACLES

As I was growing up, I believed that the only way people encountered God was through a miraculous apparition or a strange miracle. I was fascinated by these things—a piece of Eucharistic bread that miraculously starts to bleed or a statue of the Virgin Mary that begins to weep. When I was in university, I remember the news reports about a window in a local hospital where an image of the Virgin Mary appeared in the condensation between the panes. By the time I made it to witness this for myself, it had been covered up because of the considerable media attention. This is how many people operate. They rush to see the presence of God in something out of the ordinary, rather than opening their eyes to the ordinary miracles in everyday life.

One Sunday in his homily, the priest at my church mentioned his elderly mother, who had just turned ninety-nine years old. Just then, the woman in the pew in front of me leaned to her friend and whispered, "Wow!" I thought, *My grandmother is nearly ninety and quite healthy. My wife's family has been known to live long. What's the big deal?* Old age is a pretty ordinary thing. Same with babies and anniversaries! Babies are born every day, and people live long enough to celebrate milestone anniversaries. I'll admit that I've tended to roll my eyes at people who ooh and aah over these events. It's not that I don't care, but they're just ordinary parts of life. It took me a while to realize that the lady's "Wow" was an appreciation of God's *ordinary* miracles!

Births, birthdays, and anniversaries are the miracles of everyday life. Shouldn't we celebrate the miracle of God forming an intricate and complex organism in just nine months? and that this creature can live for nearly one hundred years? It's amazing! Indeed, these things are ordinary—they happen all the time. But that doesn't make them any less miraculous. The hand of God is not less present just because they are ordinary. One could argue that the very unordinary instances of winning the lottery or beating the odds against advanced cancer are miraculous. Sure, they may be. Maybe God's hand was in these things, or maybe not. But when we look only to the unusual for God, we miss God in the common, everyday occurrences around us. The last time you looked at a sunset or a playing child, did you not sense in your heart something stirring that captivated you? That sensation may be God reminding you of the miracles of the everyday.

The sun rises and sets every day. Babies are born every day. And priests take out the trash every day. These are signs of the incarnation: the things God sanctifies and which point to God.

Back when St. Ignatius was in his own search for God, he sat on the banks of the river Cardener in Spain, where he experienced a profound moment of God. His autobiography says that "the eyes of his understanding were opened." I believe Ignatius had, in that moment, an insight of God's ordinary miracles, a God moment. I think he was captivated by the fact that all he had learned and experienced before—the ordinary stuff—now had miraculous meaning, divine meaning. Joseph Tylenda, S.J., a commentator on Ignatius's autobiography, says, "[Ignatius] now perceived everything in its proper relationship to God."[10] Everything was no longer ordinary and plain; it was awe-filled and miraculous because it came from God. The "Wow!" from the woman at church, then, was a brief, audible appreciation of ordinary miracles.

Most of us slide into and out of our days without much notice of such miracles. Instead we obsess about the extraordinary miracles that make the stuff of religious or scientific documentaries. The Discovery Channel is always showing programs about the DNA analysis of the Shroud of Turin. My students tend to ask questions about bleeding hosts or exorcisms. We're captivated by the *extraordinary*. Quite possibly the saddest part of our existence is being oblivious to the *ordinary* sacred mystery around us. If each human being on earth could truly be amazed by the cosmos—how a plant converts sunlight into chemical energy; how our planet lives in a galaxy of hundreds of billions of stars and how this galaxy is one of nearly 200 billion other galaxies; or how the human body forms another person from just two cells—I'm sure there would be less hatred and violence because there would be a greater reverence for the awesomeness of life. Things that are so normal to us have mind-boggling intricacies.

Time began 13.8 billion years ago when the universe took form. Earth didn't begin to form until 9.3 billion years later. And it took *another* 4.5 billion years for modern humans to appear. Let's take a step back into the Christian mythical beginnings of creation to get a feel for a God who loves so deeply the material creation.

"In the beginning, when God created the universe, the earth was formless and desolate. The raging ocean that covered everything was engulfed in total darkness, and the Spirit of God was moving over the water" (Gn 1:1–2, GNT). Soon after that, God created light and the sky. All that existed was the mighty power of God pulsing through the infant creation. Remember how, after each step of creation, God says that it is "very good" (Gn 1:31, NRSV)? There's a sanctity to the ocean and sky and the light and darkness. The entire natural world—all the elements and animals and creatures—is imbued with a miraculous character.

One place I see God in the natural world is on the open ocean. My family has taken me on several cruises, and most itineraries have had days at sea. Around the ship is nothing but ocean and sky. At first, it's a bit foreboding. Out there you need a lot of trust in God. You hope the ship stays afloat—there's no one around, at least not in the twelve miles visible to the horizon. You also hope the desalination system, the only supplier of fresh water, doesn't fail. And the nearest solid earth may be seventeen thousand feet below you.

But this smallness that's felt after just a brief gaze out on the waters leads to a real feeling of the presence of God. All you see is ocean and sky, water and air—two "elements" of sorts. Even the clouds are a form of water. Perhaps this is what the earth looked like in its early stages as told in the Genesis story.

As creation continued, more and more came into existence, and through the centuries humankind has assisted in that creation with progress and transportation and technology. And as we continue to build up the external world around us, we try all sorts of things to make sense of the struggles in our bodies and souls, those internal things that gnaw at us day after day. God is there, but when I look out to the horizon in the middle of the ocean and all I can see is water and sky, I'm reminded of my smallness. Yet the broad and simple brushstrokes of water and sky at the beginning of the creation story give way to the tiniest brushstrokes, which include you and me in our uniqueness. Our existence is sacred and mysterious yet so ordinary. God is an artist who cares for the smallest of details. We have only existed for the tiniest fraction of the history of time, yet our God cares to be so intimately involved in our lives. Later I will speak about how exactly God gets involved with us—and not just through the birth of Jesus. God is involved with our lives right now. But we shouldn't see God as a puppet master who preordains everything. God doesn't cause you to make one decision over another, just as God doesn't cause natural disasters. The creation story we just touched on is continuing right now. Built into our world and us is the gift of free will. As hurricanes are formed through the "free will" of weather patterns, our life choices and everyday actions are made through *our* free will. Yet, mysteriously, God is involved.

GOD IN THE MESSINESS

If God chose to take on skin as a human being, that means God took on human suffering. But why do bad things happen to good people? This is certainly an age-old question, to which the best answer I think is "Why not?" Why did my closest family friend die of breast cancer? Why do tsunamis wipe out whole populations? Because it happens. There are many phenomena in the world that are as natural as death. Earthquakes, floods, and tornadoes are natural parts of our planet's ongoing creation. Disease, cancer, and famine are often natural occurrences that do not originate with some evil power. They just happen. I learned as a chaplain that when patients questioned why they got a stroke or a terminal illness, all I could say was, "I don't know." My friend's cancer was not because of some evil force. On the other hand, there do exist structural and political evils that *cause* bad things, such as lack of food or health care. Life contains all sorts of occurrences that disrupt our plans. We get in car crashes, have bad teachers, hurt ourselves, and even experience the grief of unexpected death. I want to touch briefly on how the uncertainties and suffering of our existence can actually be a source of grace, whether or not evil is behind them. God can be found amid the chaos and messiness. Yes, even through our experiences of suffering, God takes on skin and becomes real for us.

For instance, the Church is a place we don't expect messiness. We expect the Church and its doctrines and liturgies to be neat and tidy. Any disorder could, God forbid, offend our piety. Yet the Church—indeed, the world—is made up of imperfect and fallible human beings. Here are two examples of how I found God in the messiness in the Church.

One Sunday I was at Mass with my wife, Sarah, and I noticed that in the first couple pews was what seemed to be a large family dressed more formally than the rest of the congregation. "It must be a baptism!" I realized. The sacrament of Baptism is a lovely ritual because it welcomes a new member of the Christian community and washes away original sin. What a *perfect* moment!

As the baby, who was about a year and a half old, was brought forward, she began to cry. This was not an ordinary cry. She was squirming in her mother's arms and didn't want her parents or godparents tracing the Sign of the Cross on her forehead. The priest was struggling to put oil on her head, too. Over the sound of the crying, the priest was practically shouting the prayers. *Good Lord*, I thought. *Could this get any worse?* I imagined the child being overtaken by an evil spirit, resisting the ritual, resisting the holy water, as if playing out a scene from *The Exorcist*! I was hoping the prayer of exorcism (part of the Baptism ritual) would help. It didn't.

After the whole ordeal was over, Sarah leaned over to me and said, "Wow, God's even in the messiness!" It was true. Amid the child's squirming and crying and the frustrations of her parents, God's grace was still present and effective. The messiness doesn't bother God!

The second example of my experiences of God's grace in messiness is when Sarah and I were the participants in a sacrament. Thankfully there was no squirming, though there were tears! Sarah and I didn't expect a perfect wedding day. We knew that things happen and that even the weather can turn at a moment's notice.

Everything went smoothly. The weather was perfect. The music was excellent. The atmosphere was truly joy-filled, and all our friends and family were there to celebrate with us. We had rehearsed the liturgy very carefully, so everyone knew what he or she was doing at the right time. The photographer was in place as Sarah and I ascended to the altar. I looked out at our friends and family and back at Sarah. Nothing could be more perfect and lovely. Sarah and I began tearing up as we exchanged vows and rings. Then our noses began to run with the tears. As we kissed, Sarah's snot got all over our mouths, and after a brief pause, we each simultaneously wiped our mouths. We, and everyone in the church, erupted in laughter, as if we were children wiping our mouths after an icky kiss. This was an example of messiness that was still graced by God, marked by the laughter of the community and even by a snotty kiss. Here I was in the very church where I had met with my Jesuit spiritual director six years earlier, learning for the first time about how to find God in all things. And on my wedding day I could see God's grace in a snotty kiss. Perfection need not exist to have an encounter with God!

Even the birth of Jesus was not so "perfect." Like any birth, there was blood and placenta, pain and crying. Jesus' life as he was growing up involved puberty, heartache, struggle, skinned knees, and a loss of friends. His ministry and eventual death were messy. *The Message* translation of the Bible speaks about Jesus this way: "We don't have a priest who is out of touch with our reality. He's been through weakness and testing, experienced it all—all but the sin" (Heb 4:15, TM). Jesus was a good person, but bad things happened to him. He experienced things all humans experience: sorrow, loss, and pain. The twelve apostles didn't have it easy either (all except one were martyred), but still, centuries later, God continues to pour out grace on the Church they helped to build.

The incarnational nature of God means God dwells within the realities of the world: in the squirming and crying, the snot, the struggles, the births, and the deaths. The presence of God exists whether or not something "feels" holy. It was known that St. Ignatius felt tremendous scruples when he experienced the sacrament of Reconciliation. Each time he confessed and received absolution, he felt he had not fully or heartily confessed, so he would go right back to his confessor. This happened over and over until he came to understand that God's grace was being given to him regardless of how he felt.

As at the wedding and Baptism, tears symbolize the messiness in the human life, which is made up of both joy and sorrow. Ignatius often wrote about the "grace of tears" in his own prayers and lived experience. He uses the word *grace* to describe these tears because the tears were a gift from God. They helped to make present his emotions in a very visible way, and they can do the same for us. In the Psalms, tears often represent a feeling of the absence of God, yet Ignatius lifts them up to the place of consolation: "It is proper to the good spirit to give courage and strength, consolations, tears, inspirations and quiet, easing, and putting away all obstacles, that one may go on in well doing."[11] What Ignatius means is that it is good and okay to shed tears, and he lists them among other things that can lead us toward God. God dwells in the messiness of tears as well as in our weaknesses.

How many times do we recognize our faults and failings? and the faults that we continue making over and over again? We cry out, like Paul, "For I do not do what I want, but I do the very thing I hate" (Rom 7:15, NRSV). Just the very recognition of our weaknesses in prayer allows God to draw us to greater strength and love. At times I consider myself as a broken egg,

messy with the yoke oozing out. Imagine every person you know
with everything exposed. You would see it all: their weaknesses,
their compulsions, their secrets, their loves, their wounds, their
joys, their fears. And they, too, could see you in all your depth.
It would be . . . messy. Can God be present in all that mess? If
anything, the example of brokenness of Christ on the Cross says,
"Yes!" Our brokenness and weakness can indeed be a sacred
place where God dwells, hoping to heal.

I can understand how we find God in these little "messy"
things, but what about the diseases, floods, and famines? What
about violence and terrorism? I think Ignatius would say that
we cannot blame God for this disaster or that—that would be
the evil spirit working—but we can look for hints of an incarnate
God within those things. God draws the good out of terrible
situations.

Consider the terrorist attacks of September 11. No loving God
would cause or condone such violence. (A side note: I believe the
"wrath" of God in the Old Testament indicates the *interpretation*
of events and stories as told by the authors of the texts, *not* the
actual desire of God to kill.) In the days, weeks, and months after
the tragedy, communities banded together and neighbors and
friends reconciled with one another. Amid awful tragedy like
that, grudges and disagreements seemed trivial.

In the book of Genesis, after Joseph's brothers sell him into
slavery and he ends up in prison, they reunite with Joseph and
repent. Despite their evil plots against their brother, Joseph
doesn't hold a grudge against them. "You plotted evil against
me," Joseph said. "But God turned it into good, in order to pre-
serve the lives of many people who are alive today because of
what happened" (Gn 50:20, GNT).

When I was a hospital chaplain, I found something similar
among dying patients and their families. Patients told me that
they wanted to reconcile old grudges with their families and even
with God. An elderly lady, days before her death, regretted not

being baptized, even though she had lived as a faithful Christian, and so asked to be baptized. I sat with her for an hour one day as she told me stories of her grandmother taking her to church when she was young. And all these years, she had felt as if she hadn't lived a perfect life. She regretted not getting baptized, not making good with God, and not seeking forgiveness. Since no priest was available, I baptized her. As I asked her the questions for the baptismal promises, she joyfully responded, "I do!" to each one. What peace that brought her!

When unarmed black people are unjustly shot, the country comes together in new ways to speak out against racially motivated violence. Victims' families and police band together in grief and help fuel a movement for social change.

All this is messy, yet God shows up in the bonds of relationships. Whether it's God's relationship with us, the relationships within our communities and families, or even our relationship with ourselves, God strengthens these relationships in the middle of messiness. Our incarnational God uses already existing events and people to bring forth grace and strengthen relationships. But we've got to be aware of that and allow ourselves to be the skin of God, to be conduits of love and grace in a very messy world.

Messiness is also a critical part of discernment, which I'll speak more about in chapter 3. Ignatius believed that there are these two forces working on us at all times, pulling us in one direction or another, like the tension between the centrifugal force of the earth, which tries to throw us off into space, and gravity, which keeps us grounded. These tensions he names as the good and evil spirits. One draws us away from God, and the other keeps us grounded and pulls us toward God.

Discernment consists of an awareness of how the good and evil spirits draw you toward or repel you from certain choices or things. If you are choosing potential career paths or trying to decide on which city to live in, these forces are acting on you and creating a certain messiness. When your feelings about something are wavering back and forth, you tend to feel a bit unsettled. Ignatius says this kind of messiness is good because it's the perfect time to discern precisely what the feelings mean and which spirit is acting upon you. God uses your body, emotions, and feelings to give you a sense of what the best choice in a given situation would be.

I like to imagine that during those many times Jesus went to a mountain or a lonely place to pray, he was reflecting on his experiences and paying attention to the tensions (and sometimes turmoil) within him. Our incarnate God uses the messiness we feel and experience as a way to guide us.

———

God is indeed in all things. The realities around us that we can touch or feel—our relationships, the natural world, the emotions within us—are God's spirit and presence reaching out to touch us, nudging us in a particular direction. We may not get the chance to touch the wound in Jesus' side like Thomas, but through concrete experience, we get an insight into who God is and who God is calling us to be. Each day we get to step into a world of wonder and activity, of creation and new chances, and of friendships and feelings. Each day God is waiting right there in the skin and fleshiness of life and is present in our midst, calling us to an exciting project for humankind.

2

PRAYER AND
SPIRITUAL PRACTICES

In the couple years after encountering Ignatian spirituality, I felt as if I had taken a crash course in opening my awareness to the presence of God around me. Scripture came alive, I noticed the ordinary miracles in everyday life, I saw God in the people around me, and I felt a certain closeness to God. It wasn't until I had my experience in the Jesuits that I truly learned how to pray.

After leaving religious life, I had the chance to teach a class of sixth graders about faith and spirituality. I showed them a picture of a boy with his hands folded, looking upward, and asked them what they thought he was doing. "Praying," they told me. "Why?" I asked. They said he was praying because his hands were folded and because of his prayerful posture. I showed them a photo of a boy on the floor, pen in hand, writing in a journal. He too was looking upward as in thought. "What's this boy doing?" I asked the class. The responses were entirely different. He must be doing his homework, they thought; he was thinking. "Could he be praying?" I proposed. "No," most responded. "Why not?" I asked. They told me he wasn't praying because he wasn't folding his hands. He was lying on the floor doing something else: writing.

For many of us, this is our image of communicating with God. Prayer is seen as a fulfillment of an obligation and as done in a certain place and in a certain posture. I know some religious people for whom prayer is about "saying" prayers. For others it is something to turn to mainly in times of sorrow or hardship. Others may thank God for their blessings but feel guilty about asking for something they need. For still others, Mass may be their only experience of prayer during the week.

I remember praying with my parents each night before I went to sleep. Sometimes we asked God to help certain people or thanked God for the day, but most times we prayed the Our Father or that classic prayer "Now I Lay Me Down to Sleep." At dinner we'd rattle through "Bless us, O Lord . . ." We'd go to Mass each Sunday, but for me it was more about saying prayers with a large group of people than having a real experience of God.

So what exactly is prayer? I wondered. Is it more than what we did at church and before bed? It took me a while to understand prayer as first and foremost my relationship with God. When I did, prayer slowly opened up my awareness of how God reaches out to me in my life, and it taught me how to bring God to others. Prayer is only as effective as how it helps your relationship with God grow. For some, God is a distant being in the clouds who cares little about their day-to-day goings-on, as I used to believe. For others, God is a bookkeeper who keeps track of their sins and the number of times they go to church or pray. I came to find God within me and also present in people around me. Knowing you're made in the image of God is important before attempting to try any new method of prayer.

It's easy for our relationship with God to be transactional. We only go to God to ask for things or to get brownie points in God's record book. Perhaps we focus solely on gaining eternal life, so we go through the motions of worship, receiving the sacraments, and "saying" our prayers in order to do what we're "supposed" to do, but our relationship with God lacks a certain intimacy.

After the Second Vatican Council in the 1960s, there was a big shift in the Church's understanding of prayer. Christians like you and me realized that we could actually have a personal relationship with God! We discovered that God actually cares deeply about every detail of our lives and that we're not as insignificant as we made ourselves out to be.

Ignatius was perhaps beyond his time by saying that the Creator works directly with the creature. He believed that God could communicate directly with us, not just through a priest or a wise figure. We already have an intimate relationship with God and an attuned life of prayer in which God can communicate with us. This communication happens through our reflection, feelings, and emotions. While our faith tradition, Church institution, and spiritual community are places where our relationship with God gets formed and deepened, it is within prayer that our relationship with God really gets personal. This understanding is what gives life to discernment, which we will explore in the next chapter.

Up until now I've spoken about incarnation more broadly—in the ways God takes on flesh in the people, things, and events in our lives. But this concept is founded on a relationship with the person of Jesus Christ. When I was a Jesuit, I had the privilege to make the Spiritual Exercises of St. Ignatius, a full thirty-day retreat of deep prayer and intimate relationship building with the person of Jesus. Ignatius designed the Exercises for regular people, to help open the door to spiritual conversion. As one meditates on human sinfulness and frailty through the life, death, and resurrection of Christ during the four parts or "weeks" of the retreat, one is deeply immersed in the loving goodness of a God who chose to become human.

But Ignatius wants to ensure that those making the thirty-day Exercises are ready for such an experience. How can you dive right into an intimate relationship with Jesus if God is a distant bookkeeper in the clouds? How can you truly hear Jesus ask you, "What do you want me to do for you?" if you feel guilty about asking God for something? Ignatius wants to ensure that retreatants truly know the intimate love God has for them before they allow their prayers to go any deeper. Childhood doesn't prepare us for this much. "Jesus loves you" is what we hear, but God remains distant and abstract. As I was growing up, I was caught up on the assumption that God was mainly concerned with keeping track of my sins rather than with loving me beyond comprehension. And my religious educators weren't always great at changing this mind-set. This is what it's like for many adults. Jesus remains a figure so out of touch with our time and experience. When we see God as one who can't relate to us, how can we trust that God cares about the little details of our lives?

The truth is, when we see the extraordinary detail of creation and the complexity of it all, we can believe that the Creator took the same care in creating us—including our gifts and talents. I believe God wishes to be intimately involved with each of us and cares so much about our lives that having a personal relationship with us is so important. Even if our prayers are as simple as praying the Rosary or partaking in the sacraments, they still are about fostering a personal relationship with God. Pope Francis so beautifully understands that the Incarnation of Jesus Christ—a sign that God wishes to have a personal relationship with us—is the very reason for prayer and devotion. He says, "Genuine forms of popular religiosity are incarnate, since they are born of the incarnation of Christian faith in popular culture. For this reason they entail a personal relationship, not with vague spiritual energies or powers, but with God, with Christ, with Mary, with the saints. These devotions are fleshy, they have a face."[1]

Prayer takes on skin! It is a means for personal encounter, as personal as sitting with a friend at a coffee shop and pouring out your heart. Such a relationship is not vague but *fleshy*!

IF IT DOESN'T WORK, DON'T USE IT

Before I share with you some suggestions for spiritual practices or prayer methods, it's important to say that if one particular approach isn't helpful for you, don't use it. If the Spirit of God works with each individual uniquely then not every prayer method is going to be fitting for your spiritual life at the moment. St. Ignatius, when discussing material things, says we should only choose "what is most conducive for us to the end for which we are created"—that is, glorifying God. This goes hand in hand with our spiritual lives as well.

Perhaps you're reading this book because you are seeking a richer prayer life and relationship with God. You may be seeking meaning or new ways of understanding the divine. The spiritual practices mentioned in the following pages certainly don't work for everyone. What I learned about prayer is inspired by Ignatian spirituality, but the great thing about Ignatian spirituality—and Christian spirituality in general—is that there are *thousands* of ways to tap into the divine. Don't get caught up on one method or another, but rather experiment and discover what speaks to you. God will meet you there.

PRECONCEIVED IMAGES

You may not be attempting to build a relationship with God from scratch. You've got some form of a relationship with God already, and perhaps you're looking to "improve it" somehow. But as with any relationship, it takes time to build trust, vulnerability, and intimacy. You cannot begin on such a journey with your old images of God. If your God is a bookkeeper or an old man in the clouds, put that away. William Barry, S.J., says, "All the gospels describe the disciples as men who did not begin their relationship with Jesus with a preconceived picture of him that was later substantiated."[2] The disciples came to know Jesus personally through their real-life experience of him. For us, prayer is a way to have a real experience of God. Our preconceived images of God can block our genuinely getting to know the divine character. I used to live with someone who was from a particular part of the country. His accent was a dead giveaway, and my head was filled with stereotypes of what people from this region were like. I had a preconceived assumption about this guy before I even got to know him, and my preconceptions inhibited me from getting to know who he really was at his core. Needless to say, we didn't get along. And when others talked about how kind he could be, I scoffed because I could not get past the images I had formed about him in my mind.

Our images of God that may have been formed in our childhood, in our churches, or in society at large may inhibit us from truly getting to know God. Ignatius knew that to come to know God personally one had to begin by having a human experience with God incarnate, the person of Jesus.

But how do you do this? How do you get to have a human experience with the person of Jesus? Many forms of prayer are one- or two-dimensional, and God remains distant; our relationship is based solely on asking or thanking, transaction after transaction. Ignatius's style of prayer involves using your imagination to place yourself inside a story. He wants us to go *into* God's story, in 3-D, because it's also *our* story.

Those who know me well know I'm a lover of everything Disney. And two of Disney's cornerstones are imagination and story. The movies and the theme parks are built on story, which begins in the imagination of a creator. Walt Disney imagined his theme park to be like a movie set, a place where you could literally step into the movies and watch them come to life before your eyes. Walk down Main Street USA, and you're transported to the turn of the twentieth century. Enter Tomorrowland, and you've been transported into the future. The characters around you come to life and even interact with you. You become part of the action. Walt saw stories not as words on a page or flat frames in a movie but as things that our own imaginations can add to and that can personally touch our lives. Ignatian spirituality sees the same with the stories in our religious tradition.

If we zoom out to the big picture, we can see our world, all creation, originating in the imagination of God. And we help in writing the story, hopefully going along with what God has in mind, though often straying from God's idea and choosing to begin writing a story that God never imagined or hoped for. So how do we know something of God's story using Ignatius's method? We can start with scripture. The Bible is filled with stories that we can not only read but also place ourselves into.

Our imagination can place us in the boat with Jesus and his friends on the stormy sea—or at the table at the Last Supper, listening in on the conversation, even participating. Ignatius says that if we let our imagination go free, not forcing it or "scripting" it, God can use it to show us something. I recall, in my own prayer, the vivid scene with Mary and Martha. I was one of their friends waiting for Jesus to arrive to raise from the dead their brother Lazarus. We spoke about Lazarus's life and how much we missed him. But then our friend Jesus came along and brought him back to life. You should have seen the tears and embraces as the four of us rejoiced.

Over time, when we interact with Jesus this way and watch how he lives his life, we begin to get to know how our God with skin works in real life. Ignatius sees this as prayer because he believed that God uses our imagination and senses to experience God. Our imaginative prayers bring God's reality to our lives. They give God skin and flesh. By imagining yourself truly interacting with Jesus, you can counteract the idea of God as a distant and uninvolved deity.

PRAYER OF THE SENSES

Have you ever had all five of your senses engaged at once? Our brains are good at tuning out certain senses depending on what we need in the moment. I was recently out listening to some live music while eating tater tots covered in cheese. I noticed, though, that the tater tots were not as flavorful as I had remembered. The loud music overtook my other senses. As my hearing prevailed, my remaining senses lessened and the food seemed blander. This happens mindlessly when we're walking in nature, looking around at the beauty, but we tune out some of the sounds. Or we focus on the sounds and miss the visuals. I may be captivated by the sunlight filtering through the leaves but miss the sound of the chirping birds. Or I may focus on the sound of crashing waves but barely notice the wispy clouds above the ocean. Only when we become more mindful about both the visual and auditory stimuli can we both see the beauty and take in the sound of the waves and the birds.

Consider also the last time a song stirred up a powerful memory. Can you remember the last time you heard a song that took you back to a different time in your life? Maybe back to your prom or a certain relationship? Don't get me started on the songs that remind me of ex-girlfriends! And then there are smells, which are even more powerful. Smells are like instant time machines. A whiff of something often snaps me back to moments spent with my grandfather or gives me the same feelings I felt at a certain time in my life.

Our senses are critical, too, for imaginative prayer. When we step inside a biblical story, Ignatius asks us to pay attention to all our senses. In the Spiritual Exercises he calls this simply an "application of the senses." If we imagine sitting with Jesus and his friends at the wedding in Cana, what do we see? What conversation do we hear? Do we taste and smell the food? What is its texture? What does the wine Jesus just made from water taste like?

Why is all of this important? Because it allows you to join in on the experience Jesus and his friends were having. Let me give you an example of the importance of our senses in real-life experiences. A couple years ago my wife and I were visiting San Francisco, and we discovered a pretty neat speakeasy. Since we appreciate a well-crafted cocktail, we made a reservation, approached the unmarked door, and rang the buzzer. After giving a password, we were let in to a dimly lit bar, which was in the guise of a private detective agency named Wilson and Wilson. The bottles lined the wall like library books, four shelves high, requiring a ladder to reach them. We were handed a folder with "the case" in it, but between the pages of evidence and photos was a menu of unheard-of drinks with handcrafted syrups and bitters.

After ordering, Sarah and I clinked our glasses in delight. At this instant I appreciated the sacramentality of the moment. I was aware of the importance of not only the nuanced taste required to enjoy a cocktail but of the sound of the clink and the Prohibition-era music playing in the background, even the sound of the bartender's metal cocktail shaker. In fact, all our senses were engaged. Each drink had a distinct scent critical to the experience, as if we were wine tasting. The lighting was dim, and the wallpaper was black and silver. The glass was cool, and the matte-textured paper menu was written in typewriter font. Even the story line made the experience: detectives with a case file meeting behind closed doors for business. But it wasn't business. It was something completely different. My senses were all being engaged by good company and good drinks. I had an awareness of my senses as a true gift, which showed me that, yes, even sensual enjoyment can be delightful to God. The very human characteristics that make up what we call "an experience" were made possible by a God who came to earth with five senses and enjoyed wine with his friends at a wedding. This is what *sacramentality* is in the Catholic tradition—the sacred palpability of the physical world that engages the senses.

As I mentioned earlier, Disney knows the importance of engaging the senses of its theme-park guests. Step onto Main Street USA in the Magic Kingdom, and you see that suddenly you're in a different time period. You hear the trot of a horse pulling a carriage under the a cappella music of a barbershop quartet. You can literally touch the horse, too, and feel its hair. Down the street you smell sweet baking confections. You can even follow the scent to the confectionery and taste one of the treats. All these add up to an experience that touches your heart and stirs your emotions.

Similarly, when Ignatius has you imagine yourself beneath Jesus' Cross, your senses stir an emotion much more sorrowful than they would without your active imagination, and you begin to share in Christ's suffering. Feelings communicate something about our incarnate God. Our senses remind us that God takes a place among the material world where beauty resides and shows itself every day.

My friend James loves to bake. When he bakes, he purposely mixes ingredients completely by hand—with no electric mixer—because for him baking is a spiritual experience. He wants the full sensory experience, to know and *feel* that he is putting his love into his creation. For him, this sensual experience of baking is like a prayer, a connection with God via the gifts of his humanness. Whether we are mixing eggs, sugar, and flour by hand or shaking up a cocktail, the senses are an easy way to connect us with the One who gave them to us. Prayer is simply a conscious awareness of that connection. There does not need to be words, just focused awareness of the moment, the feelings, and the experience.

Below is a suggestion for a sensual kind of prayer that engages three of your senses.

Touch: Find a comfortable place to sit upright, feet on the ground. Take three slow breaths and close your eyes. Notice your feeling of touch. Feel the pressure of the seat against your bottom, the pressure of your feet against the ground, the weight of your shirt on your shoulders. These small things help hone your focus.

Hearing: Keep your eyes closed, and change your focus to your hearing. I like to visualize a spectrum of audio beginning at the left of my hearing range, continuing in front of me, and then ending at the far right of my hearing range, like a rainbow of audio. I begin noticing all the sounds coming from the left side of the spectrum, sounds close by and those distant. I hear them without judging them and then slowly move my attention more and more right, just noticing the richness and depth of all the sounds coming to my ears from that direction. You'll begin to notice that there are a lot more sounds than you realize. There's not just the sound of a passing car but chatter from people, a baby crying, footsteps, the whoosh of the breeze. Again, there is no judging or explaining or labeling, just hearing. Continue your focus all the way to the right side of your hearing spectrum, and then pause.

Seeing: Now open your eyes. Just as with the audio spectrum, there is a visual one that goes all the way from the left side of your field of vision to your right. No need to move your head; just see what you see. From the left to the right, let your eyes soak in the multitude of colors and shades and shapes. You may notice movement of people or flowers swaying in the breeze. Again, don't try to explain or label or figure out. Just see, from left to right, all that is going on in the visual spectrum.

This sensual prayer puts you in touch with something so real and sacramental that God cannot *not* be a part of it. This is your chance really to notice the amazing sensual beauty God has given us. As the psalm says, "Be still, and know that I am God!" (Ps 46:10, NRSV).

THE PARABLE OF THE EVERYDAY

I've often kept a regular journal of my experience of God. I noted the ways I found God in my everyday choices, in my prayer, my work, and in my personal life. After some time and reflection, and even a retreat, I realized that my journal became a collection of stories that were a continuation of the stories in the Bible. The scriptures are stories of everyday people who had extraordinary encounters with God. The same held true for me. The graces and God moments I recorded in my journal were a continuation of the story that began in the scriptures. Jesus' message and mission continued from his time, through his followers, to me.

Each day holds for you and me important parables that can teach us. In a prayer Pedro Arrupe, S.J., once wrote addressed to Jesus, Arrupe said to him, "With a knowledge of everyday life you could offer parables that everyone understood." For us, what better way can we understand than from lessons learned through our own real-life experiences? St. Ignatius spoke of God as a schoolteacher. From this point of view, we can see that the "parable of the everyday," like the parables of the Bible, connects us to a deeper understanding of God (and of ourselves).

One of the best ways to encounter God in the everyday is by using a method Ignatius originally meant to be used in the context of prayer. Before every prayer period, he says, we must ask God for a grace—something we need and desire. This grace should be something we can feel, such as joy, sorrow, hope, or courage. And it should be relative to the kind of prayer we're about to do.

For example, if you're using imaginative prayer to pray with the story of Christ's Resurrection, you should ask God to allow you to feel joy. If you're praying with the various stories of Jesus' life and ministry, you may want to ask for the grace of a deeper understanding of who Jesus is. When you're finished praying, reflect back and ask yourself, *Did I get the grace I asked for?*

You can expand this practice to your daily activities so that your entire day is framed by asking God for a grace and then reflecting on whether the grace was given to you. For me this begins in the shower at the beginning of my day, a place when I'm alone with my thoughts. I notice various tensions within me, hopes for the day to turn out a certain way, feelings I wish to get rid of, and events I'm looking forward to. This is a chance to ask myself, *What do I really need today? What do I really desire?* And then I simply and earnestly ask God for that particular grace. It's left in God's hands.

One time I was a bit stressed with my graduate-school classes as work was piling up as usual. One morning, the grace I asked God for went something like this: "God, today I just want to feel joyful and affirmed in my hard work and to feel that doing this theology program is worth it." That day I got some great news that some previous credits would transfer in, I got an A on a challenging midterm exam I had worried about, and I thoroughly enjoyed my two back-to-back classes. Was this a fulfillment of the grace I had asked for that morning? Yes! But I didn't really notice this until the end of the day, when I recalled the grace I asked for that morning. In my reflection, I saw how the various events and feelings I held that day truly confirmed the grace.

What this practice does is make your entire day a *prayer*. By reaching out in need to God in the morning and then at night reflecting on how God may have responded to your request, you can connect the loop of an involved and personal relationship with God. You're inviting God to be intimately involved with your daily actions. Later, you look back and see just how God might have been there in the midst of your activity. Your day becomes a parable narrative that illuminates some sort of encounter with God.

More recently, I had a job interview coming up that I was nervous about. On the day of the interview, I asked God for the grace of confidence in myself. Later, when I was driving, I listened to a podcast that spoke about our unique God-given talents and how God uses them. Just then I realized that the grace I had asked for was received! I had no reason not to be confident in my gifts and abilities. If I could best use my talents in this job I was applying for, the interview would be fine! It was as if God used the podcast to remind me that I could be confident in my abilities.

The reason I use the language of "grace" is to acknowledge what God gives as gift. Grace is always free gift from God and can manifest itself in many forms. On the surface the fruit of a grace may seem invisible, but upon reflection one may discover that a grace asked for a month ago was somehow fulfilled. It may have been fulfilled in a small feeling you felt, in a smile someone gave, in a new insight you received.

Graces—certainly in Ignatius's terms—are typically things that can be felt. You can't ask for the "grace of winning the lottery," but you can ask for the grace of feeling rich in love. You can't ask for the "grace of a job promotion," but you can ask for the grace of a deeper appreciation for your work or vocation. Those kinds of graces can be felt internally. Keep a journal of graces you ask for, and you'll start seeing how God works in your life, cares for you, and provides to you what you need as free gift. You'll begin seeing how your very life becomes a parable that you and God write together. It's a story that illustrates your encounter with God and God's deeply personal involvement in each moment of your life. That is prayer at its best.

THE EXAMEN

The examen, otherwise known as the examination of conscience, has been essential to my growing ability to recognize how God takes on skin in my daily life. Christians had been making examinations of their conscience long before Ignatian spirituality, but Ignatius popularized it. The examen is all about awareness. Think of it as reviewing your day with God. You and God sort through all the pieces, events, encounters, feelings, and emotions you experienced. All that sorting and sifting opens up your consciousness so you can better see God's active participation and invitation in your daily life. And this kind of prayer can take just five to ten minutes.

The spirit of a reflective disposition is often inspired by Mary, the mother of Jesus. Luke's gospel says, "Mary kept all these things, reflecting on them in her heart" (Lk 2:19, NABRE). She does not only think about "these things" that are going on in her life, but she makes her heart a home for all her experiences and emotions. In doing so, she's able more clearly to see God's active role in her life and to hear God's call. The verse from Luke gives a sense that Mary is not rushing through her interior examination but doing it with care.

Ignatius's examen consists of five steps: (1) express gratitude to God for the gifts you received today, (2) ask for the grace for awareness, (3) review your day in detail, (4) ask God for forgiveness for the times you sinned, and then (5) amend to do better tomorrow. Why the focus on sin? Ignatius strongly believed that there was not only a good force acting on him (God) but an evil one. When he strayed from God, it was a sign that the evil spirit was lurking. The daily habit of the examen gave him insight into how exactly the evil spirit attempted to get him off track. It also showed him the ways the good spirit works to draw him back to God.

There are many adaptations of the examen, from as simple as naming a high and low point of your day to an "extended examen" that reviews an entire year or lifetime. But typically, the examen looks over the last twenty-four hours. This kind of prayer can have a great effect on your relationship with God, your inner peace, and on your decision-making ability. I've created my own version of the examen that has been especially helpful for me, as described below.

Presence: The first step to prayer is recognizing God's presence. Ignatius says to take a moment and become aware of God gazing at you (see more in the section "The Power of Ritual" on page 51). Here you're inviting God into the prayer time. You may be approaching this examen in a very prayerful state, or you may feel rushed and preoccupied. Either way, the very fact that you have a desire to pray indicates God's presence. You can trust that since God becomes incarnate in our lives, that incarnation happens in our feelings and in our desire to pray.

Review: Step two is the classic element of the Ignatian examen: the review of your day. At this point you reflect back on all the events and happenings of the last twenty-four hours. What did you do? Whom did you meet? What were your joys? What were your challenges? Remember that, since God is looking with you, it's important to talk to God about what your day was like. Ignatius believed we could be so personal with God that we could speak to him the same way we speak to a friend. So in the same way you would tell a friend about your day, you can do the same with God. Does God know everything that happens in your life? Of course. But reviewing your day with God builds a relationship based on sharing, empathizing, and listening.

This review of your day's events is not solely focused on your feelings but on where God showed up or where God felt absent. Like Ignatius, you might focus on how the good and evil "spirits" might have been at play. You might consider how you went about making various decisions and which spirit was influencing them. How were these spirits at work in your interactions with others?

Feelings: In step three, you focus on your feelings and emotions, since they're so indicative of how we experience the world. In the past twenty-four hours, you likely experienced a slew of feelings—joy, sorrow, delight, heartbreak, anger, peace—which may seem chaotic at first. Recall those feelings and express them to God. Since the examen is a sorting through your day *with* God, God wants to experience those feelings the way you did. But you might ask, "How can a distant God know how *I* feel?" The very fact that God became human in the person of Jesus Christ proves just how much God cares about what it's like to be human. Jesus, just as any other human being, experienced thousands of feelings and emotions in his lifetime. God knows the human condition, and as your Creator, there is no one more empathic.

One Feature: Step four is the most important step for me. At this point you've taken account of the events of your day and the feelings you experienced. During this time you may have noticed one feature of your day that you kept going back to or that was calling for your attention. It could have been an interaction, a feeling, or something that happened. Is there one thing that seems to be calling you to examine it a bit more? This is often something paired with some sort of stronger feeling, positive or negative. It may be a conversation or interaction you had that left you feeling unsettled. Or it may be an experience that gave you an uplifting feeling of gratitude. Whatever calls to you, step four gives you an opportunity to pray more with it.

Ignatius calls this a "repetition." A repetition is praying again with something in which we feel there might be more to discover. Repetition offers a unique invitation to discover more about how God is actively touching our lives. When we discover deeper meaning in an experience, that discovery is an uncovering of the good and evil spirits' movements. As you pray with that one feature of your day, ask yourself, "What might God have been showing me through that experience?" You may also want to ask how God felt during that particular moment.

Magis: The final step of my examen is based on Ignatius's final step, where you look forward to the next day. I title this step *Magis*, which is Latin for *more*. After all the prayer and review you've done, you ask yourself, *What more can I do for God? What more can I do in my daily living to draw closer to God and to have greater awareness?* This fifth step of the prayer ends on a hopeful note, where tomorrow offers another chance to encounter God again in a new way.

Through regular practice over time, these five steps will become a natural conclusion to your day. More importantly, there is a mutual "getting to know you" between you and God. And as the relationship deepens, you'll learn how God becomes incarnate in the moments of your day. You will begin to recognize God's presence and activity in the moment and as it happens. When I know that God is active in even the tiniest moments of my life, I find an inner sense of peace and trust, knowing that God's got my back and that continuous reflection will help me live my life more fully because God is at my side.

The examen is not only the Ignatian building block for deeper awareness; it's the building block for discernment, which I will discuss in detail in the next chapter. Making important decisions in the light of a relationship with God requires a keen awareness of your interior motivations, your desires, and your situation as well as a knowledge of how the good and evil spirits work. Using the reflective power of the examen often will help make your future decision-making much easier.

THE SACRAMENT OF THE PRESENT MOMENT

Our brains have this amazing ability to travel in time. We're good at looking back onto past experiences to learn from them. This helps us make corrections and has the preventative benefit of helping us to avoid future mistakes. We're also good at traveling into the future, playing out scenarios in our minds of what could happen and anticipating future events to help us deal with challenges to come. We might also find a joyful excitement about events we're looking forward to.

Since our brains are naturally adept at this time travel, it's no surprise that our prayers often take us to the past or to the future too. Reflecting on our past experiences is an essential tenet of Ignatian spirituality. Only by looking back can we recognize God moments that we didn't first see in the moment. We notice certain feelings and reactions more clearly. The examen prayer is based on this looking back, but it naturally concludes with a looking forward. How can my past experiences, feelings, and reactions inform my future? What more can I do to contribute toward God's desire for the world? Ignatian prayer makes an endless cycle of looking back and looking forward, reflecting and acting, learning and applying that learning. This is where the term "contemplatives in action" comes from: a continuous cycle of allowing your reflection and examination to inform the next actions you take. If all you do is *do, do, do* but you never stop and reflect on how all you've done has been effective or has been in collaboration with God, then your doing will eventually become ineffective and stagnant. On the other hand, if all you do is dwell on nostalgic past memories or past mistakes and you don't apply what you've learned to your life, then any movement forward will also become ineffective and stagnant.

When I was just about to enter religious life, I reflected back on the years of faith formation my parents and teachers had given me. I thought about the influence of my brother, my former girl-friend, my Christian friends, and the prayer experiences I'd had. I reread parts of my journal, and I could see a thread that was leading me to where I was. God had slowly been nudging me here. My reflection affirmed my decision to take a risk and enter the Jesuit novitiate. There was a time when I saw this thread but chose to ignore it. Many of my Jesuit brothers had also ignored the important feelings and experiences of the past for a time, some putting off action for years. Being a contemplative in action is about noticing how your past informs the choices you make for the future. As I went through my Jesuit formation, I continued to reflect, letting my experiences shape me, eventually realizing that my prayers, experiences, and feelings were showing me that, as I looked toward the future, I could serve God even better as a married person.

St. Ignatius likes to frame this reflective looking back and active looking forward in three questions: *What have I done for Christ? What am I doing for Christ? What more can I do for Christ?* Since the entire purpose of life for Ignatius is to contribute to God's plan for the world, these questions are astoundingly straightforward, yet profoundly thoughtful. To use more modern phrasing: *How have I played a part in making this world a more loving place? What more can I do to make this world a more loving place?*

Ignatius's three questions set a model for prayer, one that respects different periods of time and places where God shows up. One question that's easy to miss is Ignatius's second question: *What am I doing for Christ?* This question doesn't lead us to look backward or forward; it brings us to the present moment. This, too, is an essential element of Ignatian spirituality. If our prayers are stuck in the past or the future and never truly become present then we're missing a vital part of true awareness.

In the book of the prophet Isaiah, God says, "Do not cling to events of the past or dwell on what happened long ago. Watch for the new thing I am going to do. It is happening already—you can see it now!" (Is 43:18–19a, GNT). God imbues each present moment with divine action. When we become aware of this, our present moment becomes a moment of prayer. It becomes yet another relational connection to God, who can seize us through each of our life experiences. In the film *Boyhood*, there's a scene where Mason, the main character, whom we've seen grow up over twelve years, is talking to a girl he recently met in school. As they look out over the beauty of Big Bend National Park in Texas, the girl says something profound: "You know how everyone's always saying, 'Seize the moment'? I don't know why . . .

I'm kind of thinking it's the other way around. You know, like, the moment seizes us."

The moment seizes us. It's like a stunning sunset or a rush of emotion. Those are moments in which we are seized and our hearts turn to God. And when that happens, it's prayer.

But we're not always overlooking a gorgeous national park or rushing with positive emotions. Sometimes our presence to the now takes a bit more attention. Can we allow ourselves to find wonder in seemingly normal things, such as tying our shoes, pushing in a chair, or watching a car go by? If we allow ourselves to be fully conscious of what is going on right now, we may find a new kind of joy in the very moment of God's creation. When Ignatius had his retreatants meditate on the Incarnation, he had them first imagine the Trinity looking down on the world and seeing everything going on in detail: births and deaths, crying and laughing, people working and relaxing, eating and feeling hunger, growing and learning. What the Trinity sees is creation at work, a wondrous rhythm of newness coming from a messy and flawed world.

The "creation of the moment" is the emergence of the various emotions within you: the beating of your heart, the insights gained from your surroundings, and even a deep self-awareness. God lurks in each of these present-moment events as much as he did in the past and will do in the future. Letting the moment seize you means appreciating what's right now and not getting caught up with what's yet to come.

So while Ignatius's three questions regard action and what we're "doing" for God, they key us in to a past-present-future mentality of relationship with God—that is, prayer. The genius of these three modes of attention is that they envelop our relationship with God in the context of time. God speaks to us through our pasts, presents, and futures. And since the past was once the present moment, and the future will become our present, the present moment is where God meets us first and foremost. It's where God always resides. When I ask you to tell me how you feel, you tap into the present moment. When I ask you what's on your mind, you become keenly aware of the *now*. Do you notice how all this happens in your body? While the past can be recorded in photographs and books, the present moment only occurs in your consciousness. Even if you hear a song that stirs up emotional memories, that emotion you're feeling is occurring *right now* in your body. When you pray, any thoughts or emotions that arise are in your present consciousness. This is a true incarnational experience of God, since the key to this is recognizing that God shows up in your most immediate experience: when you feel joy while conversing with a friend, when you suffer a heart break, or as you watch a child playing and share in the child's wonder.

This is what many call mindfulness. You open up your awareness and *notice*. Many religious traditions employ this, but Ignatian prayer can't exist without it. When I was younger, I never would have considered this mindfulness as "prayer." But since prayer is ultimately about how you connect to God, it need not solely take place in a church or on your knees or using a certain formula.

One time while I was driving back from the grocery store, I stopped at a traffic light and looked at the car next to me. A golden retriever had its head out the window, and we made eye contact. The dog seemed to acknowledge my existence. It was an oddly profound moment because it was a reminder that God acknowledged my existence through creation. It was a God moment. When we develop a keener awareness of the present moment, I find that we interact with God more often than we would otherwise. And when we reflect back on our experiences— like a simple moment with a dog—we see even more of God show up here and there. When I make daily reflection a habit, I actually become more aware of how God shows up in the present moment. I'm also more aware of those graces I've asked God for.

THE POWER OF RITUAL

What's the first thing that comes to mind when you hear the word ritual? Maybe habit? Rote? Robotic?

Ritual is an important part of our lives: from blowing out birthday candles to having our morning coffee to attending Mass. Rituals offer meaning and give a certain sacredness to life's actions. Ignatius says that before we pray, we ought to make a small ritual act of reverence: "A step or two before the place where I have to contemplate or meditate, I will put myself standing for the space of an Our Father, my intellect raised on high, considering how God our Lord is looking at me, etc.; and will make an act of reverence or humility."[3]

Rituals give meaning to what we do. Consider the social ritual of raising our glasses to make a toast or the religious ritual of blessing ourselves with holy water as we enter a church. These small acts orient us to the significance of what is taking place. When we engage in prayer, we're engaging in communication with God, a significant moment. By preluding prayer with a small ritual act, such as making the Sign of the Cross, playing a song, or even taking a brief moment of silence, our hearts and minds slow down and shift our gaze to God.

I made a silent eight-day retreat a few years ago, and the retreat house had several teapots you could borrow for tea. Every afternoon after lunch I took a teapot, dropped in a tea bag, filled the teapot with hot water, sliced a lemon and dropped it into the pot, added some sugar, put the cover on, took a teacup, and went to a cozy chair to pray. This daily ritual gave me much enjoyment, and my prayer felt more meaningful. In fact, a recent study showed that those who engage in rituals find their experiences enhanced. Participants were asked to eat a chocolate bar, but those who engaged in a prescribed ritual of breaking the bar, unwrapping it, eating half, and then unwrapping and eating the other half reported that the chocolate tasted better than those who simply ate the chocolate without a ritual.

We all yearn for ritual. When the Duke and Duchess of Cambridge got married in 2011, an estimated 300 million people around the world watched their wedding ceremony online and on TV. That's almost three times the number of people who watch the Super Bowl each year. Leading up to the day, news outlets and websites were obsessed with royal ritual, symbolism, and gestures. Ritual is a language that speaks to us. And when it's in the context of prayer, it becomes a language God uses to speak to us.

Margaret Bullitt-Jonas, in her book *Holy Hunger*, speaks of her struggles with overeating. During an experience at a Good Friday service, the ritual gestures allowed her to set aside her thinking and rationalizing. The liturgy somehow let her face the pain of her eating addiction. She felt invited into the brokenness and darkness the Good Friday liturgy stood for and drew personal meaning from Christ's death giving way to new life. And at the Eucharist, she felt Christ speaking to her through the language of food, calling her to greater wholeness. "All I knew was that a hunger in my body, in my soul, was awakening and finding 'speech' through the movements of a liturgy."[4]

God takes on skin through the language of ritual. Consider the rituals that are a part of your daily life. What do you do when you wake up in the morning? What are your mealtime rituals? Cultivating meaningful rituals can offer a path to inviting God into your daily actions. Make a bedtime ritual. Pray the examen. Journal. Look ahead to the next day and consider what you need from God for tomorrow.

Let me give you an example of a beautiful Tibetan ritual Rachel Naomi Remen shares in her book *My Grandfather's Blessings: Stories of Strength, Refuge, and Belonging*. You take a small bowl and slowly fill it to the brim with water. Remen says, "As the bowl fills, you reflect on the particulars of your life, whatever they are. The people with whom you share your time, your state of health, whatever problems you face, what skills and strengths you have, your disappointments and successes, your worries, your personal gifts, your personal limitations, your home, all your possessions, your losses, your history as a human being. As the bowl fills, you receive your life openheartedly and unconditionally as your portion."[5] All this, Remen says, is your "portion." It reminds me of the words in Ignatius's *Suscipe* prayer, "All that I have and hold"—our liberty, memory, understanding, and will. After you fill the bowl to the brim, you carefully carry it, without spilling any water, to a special place in your home; and as you place it there, you dedicate the contents to love and service that day. And why not dedicate the contents to God as well? Returning to Ignatius's prayer, we see the contents as gifts from God, things that help us in our path to God. "To you, O Lord, I return it," the prayer continues.

The water represents everything that you call your own, and while many of those things can seem dark and cloudy, the clarity of life-giving water in the bowl reminds us that those things are hallowed before God and can be transformed into the tools of love and service. At the close of the day, you empty the bowl outside into the earth, ready to be filled again the next morning.

Here a ritual takes the form of a sacred prayer rich in symbolism and meaning. The language of God comes through and speaks. Just like with the examen, you present all the pieces of your life before God and offer them to God.

———

Many Ignatian prayer methods invite us to a connection with God that is strikingly physical and concrete. For prayer to become an intimate connection with God, it needs to become more than a mindless reciting of words. Prayer for me has become an encounter with the God who enters each moment of my life. It reminds me that God is not distant but in the here and now.

God encounters us in our bodies, our senses, our experiences, and our imaginations. And all this happens in the constancy of the present moment. The divine presence is encountering you *right now*, in the ways these words stir you and in the plans you're making in your head for your spiritual life. And when you put this book down, this friend will be waiting for you at the next moment, the next ritual, the next person you see. As you invite the Lord into the rhythms of your day and create new habits of prayer, you'll find that your entire day becomes a prayer, and you will become much more attuned to hear the voice of God emanating through the medium of the created world.

During my two-year Jesuit novitiate, I was sent away to be a hospital chaplain in Washington, DC, for five months. I found myself struggling to find time for the intentional prayer I was so used to in the novitiate. I was too sleepy in the morning, and by the time I got home I was exhausted. I told my spiritual director I was struggling with this, and so he asked me where I saw God in my day, what I did, and if I felt close to God at all. I said, "Well, I listen to some Christian music on my walk to the hospital each morning, which gets me ready for the day. And many of my patients are often on my mind—I ask God to care for them. Many days I actually journal about how my ministry is affecting me and how I feel as if my encounters with my patients really bring God's presence to me."

My spiritual director paused and said, "Sounds like you're praying quite a lot." It was true. I was having a relationship with God, but I wasn't fully aware of it! My routine had become a kind of natural prayer, with God speaking to me through my patients, in the music I listened to, and even in my journal writing. "Find the prayer that's already taking place," an Ignatian spiritual director once told me. Prayer is hearing the voice of God in the everyday.

3

DISCERNMENT

Prayer has been the most important tool in helping me figure out how I can be God's conduit in the world. Prayer led Sarah and me to say that our purpose in getting married was to change the world—or in other words, to allow God to take on skin in us and bring about positive change to the hearts and minds of others. One might call this "God's will."

What is God's will for my life? What does God want me to do? What is my divinely inspired vocation? These are great questions and indicators of a strong and convicted faith, but what these questions do is put all the pressure on God. Don't get me wrong. How God wants me to live my life is paramount, but I can't dismiss my own role in determining what path I end up taking. I may somehow come to the conclusion that God is calling me to go to nursing school, but if I am resisting, and my resistance is more than simple fear and instead based on a complete lack of desire to become a nurse, then why should I go to nursing school? If I choose to go, I will be disregarding my own desire in order to fulfill some religious expectation that I must be obedient to God's will at all costs. Why enter a career where I will find no joy?

My father may be insistent that my divine call is to continue the family business of home construction. I may feel a sense of obligation to him and figure that this is a vocation God must want for me. And how can I disobey the fourth commandment? But if I can't hammer a nail or cut wood then why enter a lifetime of work I'm not good at? God's will for us manifests itself in our gifts and abilities, our interests and desires, as well as in the needs of others. If we are to become God's skin—God's hands and feet—in the world, then why would God call us to something without consulting us first? This is discernment.

Discernment is a form of decision-making that involves God's desires and my desires. It happens through prayer, attentiveness, experimentation, and conversation with those around you. *Desire* can be seen as a negative word, a selfish word. When we're growing up, we're often told to put aside our wants for something more important. But St. Ignatius would say that our desires and God's desires should align. Our wants *are* important! We're not talking about surface-level wants and desires, such as a desire for a particular food for dinner or a desire for a weekend trip. We're talking about deep desires, such as for relationship, purpose, vocation, service, and way of life. Discernment helps us uncover those deep desires that God also shares.

Two of the most difficult discernment periods for me were choosing to enter religious life as a Jesuit and later choosing to leave. After two and a half years as a Jesuit, I felt a strong desire for marriage. It had existed in some form throughout my time as a Jesuit, but it was something that wouldn't let go. Throughout the whole discernment process, there was a voice in me saying that leaving my current vocational path would be selfish, that my desire for marriage was selfish, that I had invested so much in this life, that leaving would be against "God's will." But through my discernment process, which involved prayer and lots of conversations with Joe, my Jesuit spiritual director at the time, I came to realize that my deep desire—my underlying *want*—was for marriage and that it was God's desire, too. Remaining in religious life could have meant remaining in a life that was not as fully life-giving as God would have wanted for me. Perhaps instead of asking about God's will, the better question to ask is, "What does God desire for me?" When we use the language of desire, we allow ourselves to explore the deeper dimensions of call and vocation.

So how does discernment actually work? It begins with what seems to be a blank page. You look out to your future and see possibilities—but lots of uncertainties. There may be two or three possibilities before you, or there may be an infinite number. You may be discerning between marriage and religious life; between careers, graduate schools, or places to live; whether or not to buy a house; or whether to do a year of service or travel. Having some uncertainty is a great place to be. Ignatian spirituality tells us that one of the best times for discernment is when we're unsure, when we're weighing our possibilities and weighing our desires.

The blank page before you can be disconcerting, causing you to flee or to freeze in fear. Discernment is the call to engage—in other words, to start filling in the blank page.

Disney Imagineers, the ones who dream up, design, create, and implement dreams in real life, *love* a blank page. It symbolizes the state of being that Ignatius says is the best time for discernment. Disney Imagineer Marty Sklar said, "There are two ways to look at a blank piece of paper. One way is it's the most frightening thing in the world because you have to make the first mark on it. The way we taught the Imagineers to think about that blank page is it's the greatest opportunity in the world. Because you GET to make the first mark on that page and let your imagination fly. It was a wonderful opportunity for all of us, and the greatest influence in my career."[1] Imagineers are all about making things a reality, giving skin to their possibilities and ideas.

Except it's not just about my imagination and dreams but God's as well! It may not seem all that spiritual, but dreams are an important first step to discerning your life's trajectory.

While discerning to leave religious life, I met with my spiritual director regularly. Joe not only listened to my experience of prayer and helped me discover how God was working but he often asked excellent questions that assisted in uncovering those deep desires within me. One of his greatest questions was, "What are your dreams?" I had never imagined a spiritual director asking that question. But what he was doing was handing me a blank page and asking me to start drawing. My dreams mattered! My dreams were actually an avenue toward revealing the incarnate God to the world.

The next weekend I made a retreat so I could continue to pray about whether or not to leave religious life. Much of my time in prayer was spent contemplating the question Joe had asked me. *What are my dreams? What do I truly desire in my life?* When I went back to Joe the following month, I told him that my dream was to get married. I imagined being a husband and a father, raising children, and still working in ministry. This was my deep desire, and over time God confirmed it. God desired it too.

Three years later, I ran into Joe at a Jesuit event, and he asked with excitement, "How've you been? Are you married now?" I could tell him yes! I am married and have found so much joy in that vocation. It is a dream come true.

Unfortunately, there are lots of things that get in the way of us reaching our dreams. Consider George Bailey in the movie *It's a Wonderful Life*. Ever since he was a child, George wanted to travel the world and be an explorer. He read his *National Geographic* magazine and dreamed of far-off places. He imagined his journeys by train and ship. He had a penchant for travel, and nothing was going to stand in his way!

What ended up standing in his way was his father's death. His father's business, the Bailey Building and Loan, was about to be bought by a greedy mogul, and the only way to save it was for George to take it over. The Bailey Building and Loan allowed the townsfolk to get mortgages at low rates, letting them have homes of their own. If George didn't save the business, people might be out on the streets. George ended up giving up on his original dreams to save his father's business. This is the kind of choice we are often expected to make. Sometimes we have to decide to give up on our dreams because there are more important things happening. It's not so easy. But what George discovered was a new dream that ended up becoming his vocation. He became a husband, father, and business owner who worked for the welfare of his community. And he found great joy in it.

For me, there were voices telling me both to stay in religious life and to leave it. "It's more important for your parents to have grandchildren," one would say. "You'll disappoint them." Another would tell me that I ought to sacrifice family and stay a Jesuit because of the priest shortage. "There are more important things!" these comments said, disregarding my own true discernment.

Perhaps the impediments to our dreams are not quite as drastic as George Bailey's. There are many things preventing us from following them. Some are more reasonable than others. Some cause us to live out our dreams in new ways, as in George's case. The first step of discernment is to consider our dreams, to start filling out that blank page, and then to notice the things that are stopping us from making those dreams a reality. Are they just excuses or genuine things to consider?

The next question to ask ourselves is, *How strong is the call to those dreams?* In the first chapter of the Gospel of Mark, Jesus calls four of his disciples. He first finds Andrew and his brother Simon, both fishermen. "Follow me and I will make you fish for people," Jesus says (Mk 1:17, NRSV). Then he comes upon James and John, who are also continuing the family business of fishing. In fact, they are both in the boat with their father. When Jesus asks them to follow him, they leave their father in the boat and follow Jesus. His call seems so powerful that I imagine they must have dove into the water and swum to shore. They abandoned their old lives and followed Jesus into the unknown.

A call to follow our dreams and desires can be unmistakably clear, as the disciples experienced, or it can be more subtle. I felt called *both* to religious life and to marriage—two *good* possibilities—but my call to marriage was much stronger than the call to religious life and priesthood. What God calls us to—and what our desires indicate—is something greater than ourselves, a project for the world that intrinsically involves our dreams, desires, abilities, and gifts. Sometimes, as with the disciples, that call requires that we abandon our old way of life (even the family business).

Since we are flesh and blood human beings, the strength of a call can often be determined by our feelings. My body can tell me a lot about how I feel regarding the possibilities before me. Perhaps there's something in the pit of my stomach that gives me caution about one choice. A pang in the heart may tell me something else. I'll never forget a powerful experience of feelings during my two-year novitiate as a Jesuit. While I was working in the hospital in Washington, my desire for married life began to grow. I even found myself falling for a coworker. There arose pangs in my heart along with doubt and uncertainty. At first I dismissed them, but one weekend I took a trip to the Jesuit community's villa house in Maryland, right on the Chesapeake Bay, and because it was graduation weekend, I was the only one there. I sat out on the dock looking over the water, watching birds soar and sailboats rock in the breeze. I put my headphones on to listen to a song by the St. Louis Jesuits called "These Alone Are Enough," which is based on the *Suscipe*, St. Ignatius's famous prayer of surrender to God. As I sat there listening, feet over the edge of the dock, the subtle pang in my heart began to grow as thoughts about married life filled my head. In my body I felt this tremendous feeling that God had even *more* planned for me—more than I could ever imagine. Was marriage a part of it? I began weeping in a mix of fear, excitement, and uncertainty. My feelings began revealing that within me there was an underlying *want*, a desire that I hadn't been paying enough attention to. When I did eventually leave and get married, it was not unintentional that the song I listened to on the dock that day made it into our wedding liturgy.

God speaks through word and experience, and we respond. But it may take a while to build up the courage to respond. Also, feelings can be deceiving, which is why careful discernment is necessary. Even important feelings may disappear for a while only to emerge later on. Feelings like the ones I experienced that day on the dock came and went. And when they went, I dismissed them as something never to attend to again. When these feelings reemerged months later, however, I knew they were something I couldn't ignore.

THE "HEART" OF DISCERNMENT: ATTENTIVENESS

In the sixth season of the sitcom *How I Met Your Mother*, there's an episode called "A Change of Heart." The story goes like this: Marshall's dad recently died because of a heart attack, so Marshall and all his friends get their hearts checked as a precaution. Barney is the last to go, and the cardiologist senses he might have a slight arrhythmia, so she asks him to wear a heart monitor for twenty-four hours. When Barney returns to the doctor, she looks at the cardiogram and questions him about particular times during his day—when his heart raced or when he had a fourteen-second cardiac arrest (you have to see the episode). The episode is a series of flashbacks based on the happenings of Barney's heart.

During the evening of that day, Barney was on a date with Nora, a girl he'd been falling for, though Barney wasn't going to admit he might have real feelings for her. Lily, his friend, who accompanies Barney at his follow-up appointment, asks the doctor what happened at 8:30 p.m., the time his dinner reservation began. We flash back to Barney waiting for Nora at the restaurant. As she walks in and he looks at her, the heart monitor on the screen seems to stop for a moment and then start up again. The doctor reacts, "His heart . . . literally skipped a beat." Lily says, "Your heart's talking to you, Barney. Do you have the guts to listen to it?"

The heart is an important organ in the spiritual life. Reading it and interpreting what it means can be challenging but worthwhile. Ignatian spirituality focuses on the importance of feelings and experiences. When I was a chaplain, my supervisor often asked me, when I expressed a feeling like sadness or frustration to point out on my body where the feeling was. Sometimes it was a tightness of my throat or an anxious feeling in my stomach, but often it was a twinge in my heart. The heart is one important place to pay attention to.

In the episode, Barney had a chance to reflect on his experiences of the last twenty-four hours but with the opportunity also to pay attention to what his heart was saying to him. When he saw Nora enter the restaurant, his heart skipped a beat. It raced in fear when Nora began speaking about marriage. These signs are important in Barney's discernment about the relationship, and that's what Lily was trying to get at. Sometimes we may think or say one thing, but our heart is telling us a deeper truth.

Ignatius tells us that we can trust our experiences and our feelings. They're more meaningful than we think. Both are ways God can communicate with us, so we should be attentive to them. God uses the physical world and our reality to guide us in discernment. George Aschenbrenner, S.J., once said, "True desire is fire in the heart."[2] Indeed, many religious and philosophical traditions see the heart as our life source. Paul Coutinho writes, "In the Bible the heart refers to the core of a person. The heart is also our emotional center and the sea of tender affections, especially kindness, benevolence, and compassion. The heart encompasses both our spiritual and psychological experiences."[3]

The expression "Listen to your heart" is a good one to live by. With enough patience and attentiveness, you'll soon be aware of the signs from God that your heart speaks to you. Butterfly feelings when speaking with a new date may say one thing, while nervous feelings before making a life decision may say another. The *heart*, the *gut*, and the *conscience* tend to be words for the same thing: a physical core within us that guides us, warns us, and points us toward one choice or another. Reflecting on our heart's feelings during past experiences gives us information for future choices.

But what about those "George Bailey experiences" we have? Sometimes our hearts seem to be pulling us in two different directions. I felt a tug toward both marriage *and* religious life. I noticed voices from within and from others that felt conflicting. One voice said that leaving the Jesuits would be selfish. Another said that I could continue ministry while being married. Another said that I needed to continue what I had committed to. These pulls in different directions are what Ignatius calls "spirits." One spirit is trying to draw you to what God desires for your life—which is also *your* deepest desire—and another spirit is trying to convince you to stay away from what's best for you. These spirits are typically termed the "good spirit" and the "evil spirit."

Ignatius offers many "rules" for discerning good and evil spirits, but they basically boil down to one thing: listen to your feelings. Think about your feelings like they are water. Water is a neutral substance. It can be used for good and bad purposes, but water is water. Similarly, your feelings just exist. What is good or bad is how you react to your feelings—feelings are not inherently bad. Ignatius offers the image of a rock and a sponge. When a drop of water hits a sponge, it's gently absorbed, but when water hits a rock, it harshly bounces back. In this sense, when the evil spirit is at work, there's a strong sense of disquiet and agitation. But when the good spirit is at work, it's a more subtle and gentle feeling, as if welcoming a friend into your home. Generally, before making a decision you want to feel at peace about it, look for a sign that the good spirit is at work.

You may be starting to realize that while God uses our bodies, emotions, and feelings to help guide us to our (and God's) deepest desires, it's not always straightforward. A lot goes on within us when we're trying to make important choices. Getting in tune with our feelings takes practice. "[Ignatian spirituality] makes you aware of what is happening inside," said Adolfo Nicolás, S.J., the Superior General of the Jesuits.[4] The question he says we ought to ask is "What happens in me?" At first glance this may seem like a do-it-yourself spirituality where no outside help is required. On the contrary, Ignatian spirituality says we are to observe all the exterior inputs (advice from others, real experiences, practical reality), see what our interior says about them (through feelings and emotions), and place all of that in the context of God. The interior response is what can indicate God's will.

Ignatian spirituality is a treasure because it is a spirituality that requires your full involvement and God's full involvement. Some spiritualties involve only self. They say that truth comes from within. Other spiritualties dismiss the self and seek only external signs of God's will. Ignatian spirituality envelops both of these things and says that one cannot work without the other. I cannot solely search within me for the answers; and on the other hand, I cannot discern what God desires for me if I do not look within. It takes time and fine-tuning to discern the signs within us.

God places great importance on us as individuals. Jesus' personal and individualized care is proof of this. Ignatius most famously said that God meets you where you are, that the Creator deals directly with the creature. This means that God takes into account your individual life experiences and circumstances, your talents and abilities, and your feelings and emotions. God may speak to you differently than God speaks to the next person. Your calling is going to be different than my calling.

Because we have such an intimate and personal God, we must be attentive to the movements of the spirits, our feelings, and our experiences. There are two ways of doing this: through opening our eyes to the world around us and through prayer.

THE "SOUL" OF DISCERNMENT: PRAYER

While the purpose of prayer is to have a relationship with God, in regard to discernment, prayer is a way we can look at the discernment process *with* God. While I've already offered some general methods for prayer in chapter 2, this section will focus on specific ways in which prayer can be used as part of the discernment process.

As I've made clear, feelings are important, but their meaning will be fuzzy unless you bring them to prayer. Another way to state this is that feelings, emotions, experiences, relationships, conversations, desires, and so on are the raw data of discernment. Prayer is where you begin sorting through that information and making meaning of it. Hindsight may also give some meaning. When I look back on my past relationships, my entrance to and exit from religious life, my meeting and marrying Sarah, and all the feelings and experiences in between, it all makes more sense now than it did when I was in the middle of it all. Consider where you are now, and look back. What were all the little details and occurrences that led you to where you are now? You may realize now whether something was or wasn't a good decision. Unfortunately, hindsight does not exist when you're in the thick of deciding whether to travel the world for a year or to settle into a career. This is where prayer comes in.

At this point you may have a decision or life choice that lies before you. But before you start sorting through the data, you want to be sure you're not trying to decide between staying at your current job and murdering your boss. The choices you're trying to make ought to be morally good things and, as Jesuits say, for the greater glory of God. So if you're trying to figure out whether or not to steal your inheritance and run off with a mistress, then you should put this book down and seek a therapist. Ignatian discernment is about contributing to God's great project, not your own.

Before you begin the meaning-making process in prayer, you should be in a place of freedom. That is, you should not have your mind made up already. You may have certain preferences, but discernment is worthless if you've already decided to become a world explorer rather than save your father's business. If both the options before you are real desires and real options, then it's ideal to be able to say, "If God is calling me to either of these options, I'm okay with that." In Ignatian language, this is called *indifference*. It's not that you don't care. Rather, *indifference* in the Ignatian sense means you care so much about discerning the best choice that you're not attaching yourself to one outcome or the other.

You have your data. You've been reading your heart. You've been attentive to your experiences and emotions. You're in a place of freedom and indifference about your choices. Now it's time to sort through it all by bringing it to God in prayer. There's no step-by-step way to go about this, but I have a few methods I've learned over the years, with the help of St. Ignatius, that can be very helpful. And remember that the number one rule of Ignatian prayer says that if it doesn't work for you, don't do it. God deals with you directly and in a way that works for you. Always give a prayer method a try or two, but if it doesn't work for you, there's no reason to force a particular method of prayer. As you begin this process, be sure to ask God to give you consolation about the best choice.

FOR LIST LOVERS

You may not consider prayer to be logical, but for those who like to make lists or see things on paper, this method can be very helpful. Make a list of the advantages and disadvantages of each choice you are discerning. Be honest, and write down as much as possible. Write down things you've learned about each choice, potential consequences of either choice, and your feelings about one or the other. You're filling up the blank page that Disney Imagineers love so much! Now cross out anything in the list that might be inspired by selfish inclinations. These things are different than deep desires. If you're deciding whether to pursue the priesthood and you write down "higher status" for an advantage, you ought to strike that from the list. Having a title or high status is not about positively contributing to God's project; it's more about you. On the other hand, if you write, "It would allow me to use my gift of listening," great! Keep it. God wants you to use your gifts!

Once you've made your list and your page is no longer blank, prayerfully look it over. Imagine God looking it over with you. Talk to God about it. Imagine looking through God's eyes. What does God see? How do you feel now that you see your choices and data on paper? A couple years ago I discovered a great smartphone app called *Feels* that simulates this process. You enter the choices that you're deciding between, note each choice's advantages and disadvantages, and then note how you feel about them. The app spits out an analysis based on your input. My wife and I actually used this app as part of our discernment of which city to move to for work.

This method of prayerful discernment certainly may be helpful in decision-making, and one could even come to a conclusion using the pen-and-paper method. However, this method is only one piece in the process. Even after sorting the data a bit and weighing your choices logically, there's more to discernment.

USING YOUR IMAGINATION

Have you ever found yourself watching a movie or TV show and verbally telling the character—who can't hear you—that he or she shouldn't be making a bad decision? You can put this idea to work in your imagination. Imagine speaking to a stranger who is dealing with the same conundrum that you are. The stranger asks you to help him or her better respond to God's call. What advice would you give to this person for whom you would want the best? In this instance, the character in the movie of your mind is someone who represents you. What are you yelling at the TV?

Or imagine yourself on your future deathbed, where you will have much more clarity. What decision would you have made? Why not go a step further while you're at it. Imagine yourself in heaven before Jesus. Your life has ended, and you're talking to him about your decision. What decision would give you happiness and joy in presenting it to Christ on the day of judgment? Remember that I'm not talking about a decision concerning what to eat for breakfast. We're talking big life choices. Of course, if all you eat for breakfast every day is donuts, then you might want Christ's input on that! Little choices often do add up to big ones.

These suggestions use your imagination in the context of prayer. One of the best imaginative prayers I used in my discernment both to enter and to leave religious life was imagining myself going before God with a choice. I would first approach God *as if* I'd made one choice. For my first prayer experience I would, for example, imagine going to Jesus and telling him that I'd decided to enter religious life. Then I would see what he'd say and converse with him about why I had made that decision. A while later, I would go back to Jesus in prayer and tell him that I'd chosen not to enter religious life and why. Again, I'd listen to what he'd have to say about that. This was very helpful for me to be able to articulate directly to God—rather than just on paper—my desires and reasons for one choice or another. And since God uses our imaginations to communicate with us, we can trust this as another helpful part of the discernment process.

Spiritual direction is also extremely helpful in processing your prayer experiences. A spiritual director may make suggestions for prayer, including relevant scripture passages, but his or her primary role is to help you be attentive to God's movement in your prayer. A spiritual director can help you discern what might be from God (the good spirit) or not from God (the evil spirit).

Slowly, the raw data of feelings and emotions begin to take shape and develop some direction and meaning. And as you bring all your data to prayer, you actually find yourself with new data: feelings and insights from prayer itself. Continue to be attentive to this information and how the tugging within you shifts (or doesn't). Remember that discernment is all about paying attention, because God communicates to us through our concrete experiences and feelings.

THE "ACTION" OF DISCERNMENT: EXPERIMENTATION

By this point you've paid attention to your heart, you've filled your blank page, and you've even used your imagination to get further insights from God about your decision. The next step is to put some action into your discernment and get a "preview" of what making a definitive choice is like. At this point you're going to ask the question, "What would happen if I *absolutely and definitively* chose option A over option B?"

THE DISCERNMENT FITTING ROOM

You've done this method partially already if you went to God in prayer saying you've chosen one thing over the other and seeing what God had to say. But now you're going to go about your daily life *as if* you've really made up your mind and come to a decision. In essence, you're experimenting with one choice. Consider it like a dressing room in a clothing store. You just don't know which outfit to choose, so you try on each of them and then look at yourself in the mirror. Except it's not just about how you look but also about how you *feel*. Does the outfit fit well? Do you feel confident in it? When you see yourself in it and wear it, does it feel like the right choice? Are you ready to decide to buy it?

Perhaps it's a simplistic metaphor, but this is what you're doing with your decision. Choose one option, and then spend a few days *as if* you've definitively made the decision. You don't have to tell anyone yet, but just act as if you've decided and see how the choice feels. Look in the mirror, wear the decision, and notice how you feel. When I was discerning to leave religious life, it was between semesters of philosophy studies. I figured Christmas break would be a great time to try on each decision for a few days. For the first few days I pretended that I had decided not to return to graduate school and that I had asked my superior to leave the Jesuits. This would mean I'd pack up and go home. I'd search for a job and a place to live. I'd date in the hopes of eventually finding a marriage partner. *Yes, this is what I was going to do!*

As I convinced myself that I had made this decision, I noticed how good I felt. I felt so excited for the future and what God had in store for me. I was thrilled to date again and to explore ways of getting into ministry as a layperson. It just felt *right*. I felt consolation, which Ignatius defines as an increase in hope, faith, and love. Consolation is a peace that comes from the love of God and our love for God.

After these few days of excitement, I was afraid to spend the next few days acting as if I had made the other choice: to spend the next two and a half years in philosophy studies and my entire life in religious community without a romantic partner. I'd continue in ministry, and certain doors would be open to me that wouldn't be open to me as a layperson. Eventually I would be ordained as a priest.

These few days were tough. And to be honest, it was hard to convince myself that I had made this decision. I noticed myself on edge, not feeling ready to return to this life. My family, with whom I was spending the holidays, noticed my agitation. I felt unsettled and a bit down in the dumps. My feelings during those few days could be summed up in one big sigh.

When the days of "trying on" each choice were over, I was pretty sure I knew that the choice I had to make was to leave religious life.

Trying on our choices in a more real way like this can be extremely insightful. Convincing yourself that you've made a particular decision and noticing what occurs within you may confirm the insights you received in your prayer. When you try on a particular decision, you ought to ask yourself, *Do I feel God confirming this choice?*

EVERYDAY EXPERIMENTATION

The idea of experimenting with various choices can be exercised in day-to-day life depending on our situations. Obviously, while still a Jesuit, I couldn't literally try on a decision to leave religious life by dating people. But those who are in a position to date can experiment with discernment. In dating, you have chances to meet and go out with various people before making any commitment to them. This is a good opportunity for discernment and awareness. Without the commitment, you can freely date without pressure and use that time for reflection, assessing what your desires and feelings are, what your needs for a relationship are, where your heart is, and what each person has to offer, practically, emotionally, and spiritually.

It may be harder to "test out" a job or living situation, but nothing has to be permanent. After some time you may realize that you are meant for a different vocation or you are better off living in a different city. This may lead you to leave your situation after a year to seek something else. These kinds of long-term situations can be the hardest to discern, but at some point taking action one way or another is the best way to move forward.

Spiritual growth can also be obtained by experimenting with different ways of prayer, daily routines, and even sacrifices. I fasted from Facebook for a month and found I didn't really miss it. In fact, I had more time for praying, writing letters, and connecting with others. The experiment had a positive result, and now I need to discern how to keep my Facebook usage low. Or perhaps I might choose to reduce coffee as an experiment to see if my physical well-being improves. It might even be a chance to grow in my ability to abstain from caffeine. Similarly, any kind of sacrifice you make may strengthen your spirit and willpower.

Experimenting is part of life at every step. It is and should be part of the way we discern, and along with it come mistakes that lead us back to the road we're meant to be on. Albert Einstein once said, "Anyone who has never made a mistake has never tried anything new." So what choice do you need to try on?

THE "CONTEXT" OF DISCERNMENT: COMMUNITY

When you imagine yourself in that metaphorical discernment dressing room, who else is commenting on your outfit? Clearly only you can make the final decision about whether to purchase it, but if you've got someone with you, you're likely going to ask for his or her opinion. Community is an important element of discernment.

As I discerned the possibility of marriage with Sarah, I began to think about how alone many couples can be in this process. Yes, they might get "vibes" from each other's families as to whether they're accepted or not, but in the end many couples discern marriage completely on their own.

Sarah and I made a point to do an Ignatian-style discernment as I laid out above. We prayed and discussed on our own, but we also made it a point to share the fruits of our discernment with our spiritual directors, to speak to close friends about it, and to discuss the relationship with our siblings and families. The discernment became not just for us but for the community. A couple's relationship impacts not only the couple and their families but also thousands of people throughout the course of their life together. Tapping into the communities they touch is critical for their discernment.

In Western society, the individual is king or queen, even if it means those kings and queens are battling it out for the "Most Individual" trophy. In many other cultures, the human person is not a person apart from his or her community. Decisions are not made for and by oneself, but they are made with the community of which one is a part.

In the Bible, after Judas died and was no longer part of the twelve apostles of Jesus, the disciples spent time in prayer together and discerned possible replacements for him. In the film *Of Gods and Men*, the monks discerned through meetings together whether to leave their monastery for safety's sake or to stay put, remaining in solidarity with the people they'd come to love in the surrounding community.

When I discerned to enter the Jesuits, I engaged in lots of prayer, met regularly with a vocation director, had interviews with Jesuits and laypeople, and took a psychological test. Finally, a board of several Jesuits discerned together that God might indeed be calling me to that life. I didn't have to discern on my own; I had many other people around me helping in the discernment of my vocation.

Others cannot make up your mind for you, but input on your discernment from those who are important to you can offer you more data to sort through in prayer. If God takes on skin and touches us through the people in our lives, then what others have to say is worth taking into account. And when we hear different voices with different opinions, those, too, need to be taken to prayer.

Discernment is being attentive to the many little parts as well as to the big picture. The contexts and communities in which we find ourselves must be taken into account when discerning where and how we will best serve God and best use our gifts. Michael Himes, a priest and theology professor at Boston College, gives three key questions to ask when contemplating various life choices. The first two questions ask if what you're doing or would like to do is a source of joy for you and if it's something that uses your gifts and talents. Himes's third question is important to our discussion of community: *Is what you're deciding on something people need?* That is, would your community benefit in some way from your choice? Who are the people that your decision would affect? He gives the example of being a shepherd in an urban city. You may be good at shepherding. It may give you joy, and you may be good at it. But if you're among people who don't need a shepherd, then it's either not the right decision or you need to go somewhere with a community who does need a shepherd.

Let me put it another way. The people in your life whom your choice would affect are worthy of including in your discernment. If you are considering moving across the country for graduate school, you ought to think about the people you'd be leaving behind. You should talk to the people who know you well. Consider the new community you'd be entering into or the people in the future whom your degree would serve. Communal discernment is more than getting opinions; it's considering the people for whom you are a conduit of God's love and presence. No decision is ever one-sided—or even two-sided. Every decision you make becomes a manifestation of God in the world.

GIVING SKIN TO OUR DECISIONS

St. Teresa of Ávila said, "Christ has no body but yours, no hands, no feet on earth but yours." When we discern God's desires for us, we become channels for God's love and grace. Our skin becomes God's skin. Our actions of love become God's actions of love. Every choice we make in line with God's desires for our lives brings God a little more into the world. Incarnation was not just one brief moment on December 25. Incarnation continues daily as creation continues to unfold and as we make choice after choice.

God's Incarnation in the person of Jesus does teach us something profound. Louis Savary says, "A primary reason for incarnation is that God wanted to reveal to us that everything God created in the universe—literally every thing and every process—is sacred and holy and lives in Christ."[5] *All* things are good, including the process and fruits of discernment. All you need to do is discern God's desires as best you can, using the information gathered through prayer, reflection, and reason.

But what if you're still unsure about which decision to make? After my prayer and discernment about leaving religious life and pursuing the vocation of marriage, there was something holding me back from making the decision. It was an endless litany of what-ifs. *What if I'm making a mistake? What if I never find a partner? What if I was blinded in some way in the discernment process?* Joe, my spiritual director, told me that this was the evil spirit working. For me, it was just a matter of having the courage to actually make the decision and tell my superior I wanted to leave.

Two years earlier, when I made the Spiritual Exercises as a Jesuit novice, my retreat director would implore without fail, at the end of every daily direction session, "Courage!" Discernment can be frightening—and so can prayer—but this single word helped me move forward and trust that God would take care of whatever was next in my life. Jesus even said, "Courage, my

daughter!" to the hemorrhaging woman who had faith enough
to come up to Jesus and touch him (Mt 9:20–22, GNT). The word
courage comes from the Latin *cor*, meaning heart, a symbol of
inner strength. The evil spirit, which was causing me to ask all
those what-if questions, was simply trying to *dis-courage* me, even
though I had the inner strength and courage to make my decision.
Courage allows us to dive in and take a risk, trusting that our
God has a hand stretched out and is saying, "Don't worry—I've
got your back."

The Nativity of Jesus can perhaps encourage us in our decision because we remember that God cares about us deeply
enough to become one of us. We can trust what our heart is telling
us because we can trust God's faithfulness—on Christmas Day
and on each day of our lives.

Our choosing to live one way or another, or to do one thing
or another, is an incarnation of God. God's will becomes present
in a new way in our lives. Sometimes a decision gives the great
feeling that *I* am an instrument of God! This is consolation. But
the process is not finished. Making a decision means we have
to live it out. Jesus' first breath was followed by about 277 million more, and during that time Jesus had to discern continually
the next steps to take. These are sometimes referred to as "calls
within the call." They are the tasks of everyday living, the choices
within relationships, the decisions to say one thing or another
or to go this place or that. These little incarnations each day can
be discerned through prayer and use of the examen (see chapter
2), and they add up to our entire commitment of bringing God
into the world.

What's important to consider with an incarnational understanding of decision-making is that *we* are the only ones who can
ultimately make decisions for ourselves. God gives us the free
will to make one choice or the other. When I was at that place of
limbo where my heart seemed to have decided that leaving the
Jesuits was the best choice but my mind was still asking what-ifs,

I felt as if I was at a blockade. Yes, my heart had the courage, but it was as if I was waiting for someone else to make the decision for me! I expected God to give me some lightning bolt of a sign that very clearly pointed in the direction my heart was leaning. Our practical human side tries very hard to seek out certainty before taking any action. We're continually weighing the risks and benefits, but when we're in a conundrum, we sometimes prefer that another person make the decision for us so we don't have to.

But if we are really God's hands and feet in the world, as Teresa of Ávila says—if we are conduits of God's action in the world—then God empowers *us* to take those actions! I could have hemmed and hawed for months, remaining in a place and state of life that was not fulfilling, simply because I failed to own my power to take action. I realized that the perfect clarity I was seeking would never come. I had to take a risk, but I had to do it in the service of my discernment and in the service of God. God was waiting for me to claim the fruits of my prayer and discernment.

When we take a risk, especially with a major life change, there's a chance the decision will end up being the wrong one. There was the risk that after leaving religious life I would regret it and discover I was meant to remain a Jesuit. We don't know these things until we actually take the step and make the choice. But making a choice requires continual freedom, a freedom where we can tell ourselves, "I have discerned as best as I can and am going to make a decision, and even if it ends up being a mistake, I know God will be there for me and continue to direct me to where I need to be." When a decision ends up being the "wrong" decision, that just means the discernment will continue. God will not abandon you. After all, Ignatius said we should be choosing between good things. I knew God would be happy whether I was a Jesuit or not. Staying in the Jesuits would not have been "wrong," but I did discover that marriage is the *best* way for me to live my life. God's gift of free will can be paralyzing, but it shows the love and trust God has in you and me to affect lives, follow our hearts, and bring God into the world. The God with flesh became all things to all people. And his Incarnation means our very choices are made sacred. Discernment is a process of incarnation, of letting God in to the everyday of our lives. The Nativity reminds us that God has already been here, been intimately involved in our lives—and that involvement isn't going to stop. Every decision we make becomes an incarnation, a little Christmas through which God enters the world.

4

WHOLENESS

We journey through life looking to discover who we're meant to be, what path we're supposed to take, and what we're supposed to believe in. As we get to know our roles in God's project through prayer and discernment, we move toward what we all desire: wholeness, our *true* selves. In other words, we're looking to discover who God made us to be. In my ministry of companioning people and offering spiritual direction, I realize that this search never truly ends. We're *all* struggling with our own brokenness and fear. We're all clinging to things that end up weighing us down. And most of us don a mask for the world that makes us look "put together." This is what many spiritual writers call the "false self." We present this false self in selecting only the best photos or shares for our Facebook profiles, in overly embellishing our résumés, or in buying only "nice" clothing and cars. We get caught up with things that don't truly define who we are in God's eyes. Giving God skin through our lives best happens when we shed the false self and reveal the true self.

Becoming who God meant us to be is often a life's work. We all have a true self within us that needs to be uncovered. Even those who've committed the most heinous crimes can come to that place of wholeness and become who God desires them to be; they just need to uncover it.

St. Ignatius lived a bit of an unsavory life. Even after he lay in bed recovering from a shattered leg in battle, he struggled with his desires for, on the one hand, a life of vainglory and gallant knighthood, and, on the other hand, a life of virtue following Christ. But as he read about the life of Christ and the saints, he realized that there was something missing from his life. He was dissatisfied. This was an invitation from God for freedom and wholeness. Ignatius wasn't called to a life of vanity. God was calling him to remove the mask of his false self and to uncover the true self he was made to be: a saint.

I'll often read about a saint or a person in the news who has changed the world in some positive way and think, *I need to become like them!* I'll see those around me who seem to have their lives figured out and try to be like them. We see it in the media all the time: people being asked, "What's your secret for a long life / losing weight / a happy marriage?" We try so hard to be *other* people that we don't allow ourselves to be *ourselves*! St. Ignatius did not become one of the saints he was reading about. He became his own saint!

JESUS AS THE WHOLE HUMAN

The Christian search for wholeness only needs to look at the wisdom of Jesus Christ. He is the ideal of what it means to be wholly human. Before God took on skin and became one of us, the philosophers separated the material and the spiritual realms. The world was seen as evil. Human flesh was seen as corrupt and depraved. The spiritual realm was a place the heavenly beings inhabited, a place that we may never reach because of our depravity. But when God took on flesh, the material world was divinized—made holy. The dualism created by philosophy could not hold up. The line between the sacred and the profane blurred. Sadly, many Christians through the centuries have maintained a harsh dualism between the material and spiritual, forgetting just how radical the Incarnation was. True wholeness (and holiness) in God's eyes can be ours as human beings.

Jesus' teaching on how we can reach true human wholeness is quite paradoxical. A grain of wheat must die in order to produce fruit, he says. We must be (metaphorically) blind in order to see. We must love our enemies. Sell all your possessions and you will be rich. Lose your life to save it.

To be Christian means to die and be reborn into wholeness.

The Ignatian principle of *cura personalis* calls us not just to care for other people but to care for ourselves as well. It calls us to be whole and integrated persons. Yet we ourselves create a dualism between the material and spiritual world, the world of faith and our private lives, the internal and the external, and even between virtues. In his book *The Road to Character*, David Brooks talks about résumé virtues and eulogy virtues. Résumé virtues are the attributes we market ourselves with publicly: team player, go-getter, physically attractive, leader, and so on. Eulogy virtues are those virtues that would be shared at our funerals: passionate, humble, generous, kind, and so on.[1] We pretend that those external résumé virtues are who we are, when in reality our whole selves include both sets of qualities.

The outwardly facing self may be part of one's false self or just part of the picture. After my wedding, I posted many of our professional photos to Facebook, changed my profile picture to the best one of me, and made my cover photo the "perfect moment" of my first dance with Sarah. Whenever something good in my life happened, like a trip somewhere or news of a new job or finishing my graduate classes (or getting a book deal), I posted about it. Anyone visiting my profile would assume that my life was all put together. Everything fell perfectly into place. It was picture-perfect. But they only saw a polished picture; they didn't see the broken side: the imperfections in my relationships, the jobs I did not get, and the struggles and occasional boredom with my writing. We all know how annoying it is when people post about that "negative" stuff, right?

We mistake perfection for wholeness. Growing into whole human persons made in the image of God means integrating our *entire* selves: the strengths and the weaknesses, the joys and the sorrows, the gifts and the imperfections. Who we're supposed to be comes only partially in our job or career. Our identity is inclusive of those strengths and weaknesses that make up who we are. Here I want to discuss those other parts of who we are in God's eyes. It is our wholeness—that is, becoming who God made us to be—that more fully reveals the incarnate God to the world.

ACCEPTING WEAKNESS

A few years ago, I discovered the Enneagram, a personality model that groups people into nine different types. What makes the Enneagram unique is that it begins with our weaknesses, fears, and compulsions. Each type focuses on a "core sin" and helps us come to a certain self-awareness so we can be freed from that sin and move toward being whole people. Ignatius similarly begins his Spiritual Exercises with a meditation on sin. We're forced to confront the reality of sin in the world, and just how broken our own sin has made us, from our youth up until the present moment. Then Ignatius says, "I look at myself as a sore and ulcer, from which have sprung so many sins and so many iniquities and so very vile poison."[2] This is quite graphic language. But he knows that, in order for us to find wholeness, we need to look at those times we've hit rock bottom. His purpose for this meditation is not to cause us to beat ourselves up (though that may be part of our coping) but to remind us that, despite how broken we can be, the angels and saints have still been praying for us; the earth "has not opened to swallow me up."[3] God still loves us, and creation continues its course.

Yes, we all have our inner demons, but that's no excuse for not dealing with them. Jesus went around driving them out of people, after all! What are their entry points? Our weaknesses. Ignatius said that the evil spirit works like a military commander who seeks out his enemy's weakest points to attack. Our weaknesses won't always go away—often they're just part of who we are—but if we're not keenly aware of them, then we're opening the door to the demons that lead us to an unhappy life.

A few summers ago, I made an eight-day retreat at the Ignatius Jesuit Centre in Guelph, Ontario. The retreat house sits on a large, active farm that grows everything from garlic to beets to carrots. I happened to be praying with the parable of the weeds from Matthew's gospel (see Mt 13:24–30). The owner of a wheat field posits that the weeds that appeared in his field were planted by the enemy. "Should we pull them up?" one of his servants asks. The master shocks them by saying no. If they pull up the weeds, they might pull up some of the good wheat with them. This parable didn't make much sense to me until I had the opportunity to help harvest some carrots at the retreat house's farm.

I made my way out to the field with some farmers and discovered that the carrots were surrounded by weeds. When I pulled out the weeds, the carrots would come out with them. And while I was pulling up carrots, I found that sometimes small carrots were buried in the dirt and roots of the weeds. You first had to search out the weeds in order to find these carrots, gently pushing aside the dirt and roots of the weeds. Those weeds could symbolize our weaknesses and limitations or those "core sins" of which the Enneagram encourages us to be keenly aware.

It took me a long time to come to know what my weaknesses were, and it took me even longer to accept that my weaknesses were simply a part of who I am. According to the Enneagram, a core sin is an inherent tendency within us that causes us to make mistakes. It's part of our identity. Just as Ignatius writes about how to counteract the evil spirit, the only way we can overcome a core sin is by being keenly aware of how it operates. And just as there's no getting rid of the evil spirit, there's no way to rid ourselves completely of a core sin tendency. In the parable, the farmer tells his workers to let the weeds grow alongside the wheat. Pull up the weeds too soon, and you pull up the fruit prematurely. If we're aware of the weeds, examine them, and observe them, we're bound to find the fruit we're looking for. Similarly, our human weaknesses and personality quirks are not going anywhere, but we still must be aware of them in order to find growth.

As an Eight on the Enneagram, my core sin is *lust*—that is, an intense desire to be in control. Why? Because the basic fear of an Eight is being controlled by others. Now, this energy can be a great power for good in the world, for leadership, for overcoming injustice, and for taking risks, but at its worst it can cause self-absorption, domineeringness, and resentment. I recall a time when the "weakness" of my Eightness made itself very clear to me. In the Jesuit novitiate, I struggled to figure out what it meant to be a Jesuit and to live in a community with seventeen other guys. One day my novice director called me into his office and told me that there had been some complaints about me and that others had perceived me as selfish. My heart dropped. Selfish was the *last* thing I wanted to be! We're often quite unaware of our weaknesses and how they affect others' perception of us. It seemed that in my effort to lead and take charge (with positive intention) in community, I came across as selfish and domineering.

For years I've struggled with the reality of my personality, which the Enneagram so vividly revealed to me. My efforts to help others and make positive change can come across as controlling, often without my knowing. I've met other Eights who struggle with this. To themselves they appear gentle and loving, but to others they can appear abrasive. I've experienced this with my family, my friends, and my wife. It's hard! Sometimes I wish God had given me another personality type! I figured that with a certain amount of effort I could take on a different personality. I could be like those people I knew who seemed to be loved by everyone and who had their lives figured out. I mistook perfection for wholeness. The hard truth is that my Eightness is a part of who I am. I can't become someone else. When I struggle with this, my wife often reminds me that my "lust" for life and the courage and confidence of being an Eight can be used for good. When I'm at my best, I stand up for others, I am resourceful, and I take initiative for good causes.

While on that retreat on the farm, my struggles with my personality type came up. "I really struggle with being an Eight," I told my spiritual director, who was familiar with the Enneagram. Finally, at the end of the retreat, I sat in the retreat house chapel, opened my hands, and prayed Ignatius's *Suscipe* prayer. "Take, Lord, and receive all my liberty, my memory, my understanding, and my entire will. All I have and call my own, you have given to me as untold gift." I paused. My Eightness was part of *who I am*, part of my identity, and God gave me my Eightness. God gave it to me as a gift! I continued, "To you, Lord, I return it. Everything is yours. Do with it what you will." I could hold up my Eightness to God, and God could use it for good! God could take what seemed to be such a weakness, such a burden, and make love manifest through it!

That moment of prayer helped me accept my Eightness, my personality, and my identity—weaknesses, weeds, and all. God was calling me not to be someone else but to be myself and to accept myself for who I was. Jesus accepted that his true self was the one whose vocation was to go to the Cross. He accepted the weakness of being broken to be made whole again. That's the incarnational reality.

I was made whole on that retreat. The Christian life is a continuous rebirth from the Cross to the Resurrection, from the plunge into the waters of Baptism and out into a new life. The paradox, however, is that despite this rebirth into a new life, our weaknesses remain. I am still an Eight, and I struggle with the consequences of that every day, but my acceptance of that helps me be more empathetic to those who struggle for justice and fairness in the world, and helps me to make amends when I come across the wrong way. When my Eightness is used for good, I more easily can be a conduit of God's love and justice.

Jesus' wounds remained even after he rose from the dead. He retained the wounds in his hands, feet, and side. In life there are many things that limit us, whether it's blindness, a mobility issue, or a personality flaw. The fact that Jesus retained his wounds when he resurrected makes me wonder, *Will we retain our limitations and wounds when we rise from death?* A deaf person may tell you that her deafness is a part of her identity. Would God remove such a core part of her identity at the resurrection? My Eightness may at times be a limitation, but it's a part of who I am. I can't imagine losing part of my identity simply because I'm in heaven!

When teaching faith-formation classes for sixth graders, I ask the students to name not just the things they're good at but also the things they're not good at. Why? Because even our weaknesses are part of who we are, and to be whole means to accept them.

Jesus had his own weaknesses as part of being human. The Letter to the Hebrews says, "We don't have a priest who is out of touch with our reality. He's been through weakness and testing, experienced it all—all but the sin" (Heb 4:15, TM). He made mistakes and fell into human ways like we do. In the garden he asked his Father if there was a chance he didn't have to go through the pain of suffering (he feared pain). He fell at the weight and pain of carrying his cross (he had no super strength). At twelve years old in Jerusalem, he didn't let his parents know he was in the Temple, and so they left with the crowd figuring he'd come along (perhaps he was enthralled in the moment? or forgetful?). He just never let his weaknesses get in the way of serving God.

He never acted in any way contrary to God's law or love of God and neighbor.

When Jesus Christ offered himself to his disciples in the Eucharist, he wasn't just leaving his body and blood to us; he was leaving his *whole* self, the one that had to grow into his vocation, accept his humanness, die, and rise. Just like Jesus, we need to accept our whole selves—strengths and weaknesses.

WHO AM I?

This is probably one of the hardest questions we can ask ourselves. Wrapped up in this is our purpose, how we choose to live out our lives, the families we grew up in, our gifts and abilities, and our very identities. When Jesus was a teenager, he was likely asking this same question. When God chose to take on skin and become one of us, God decided to take on the human need to learn. Jesus' humanity meant he had to learn his ABCs just like the rest of us. He spent time in the Temple asking questions to the rabbis. He learned a craft from his father Joseph. Over time, Jesus grew into a fuller understanding of who he was: the Son of God.

We tend to start articulating the question "Who am I?" in our high school years. Then in college our interests start solidifying, and we experience new kinds of friendships. We test the waters of life by asking questions and by challenging our beliefs, deepening our understanding of ourselves and the world around us. But this wondering about our identities does not stop after the age of twenty or thirty. In fact, we may find ourselves asking this question until the day we die.

Ignatian spirituality assists us in discovering our identities in God, our purpose. Ignatius truly saw each person created by God as a part of God's plan for the world. He would say that we are cocreators with God in the unfolding creation of the world and universe. St. Ignatius's thoughts are paraphrased well by author Louis M. Savary: "You were created to make a unique contribution to the great evolutionary project initiated and continually supported by God, namely, bringing all creation together into one magnificent conscious loving union. . . . And God is with you as you undergo whatever diminishments may befall you as you cooperate with others in your efforts and actions in pursuing this divine project—the purpose for which we, individually and collectively, were created."[4] So how do we uncover this reality? How do we discover our true identities?

Les Misérables tells the story of Jean Valjean, whose petty crime resulted in nineteen years of imprisonment and hard labor for him. Valjean was then released, but after breaking the terms of his parole, he lived a hidden life, took on a new name, and started over. Throughout the story he struggles with his past and continuously tries to hide it from himself and his adopted daughter, Cosette. Ultimately, he comes to realize that he cannot run away from his story and reality. It has made him who he is.

Jesus lived his life never hiding the reality of himself and of God's kingdom. Despite the suffering he would endure, the embarrassment the Pharisees might feel, or the pain of the truth that we're all sinners, Jesus was dedicated to uncovering reality at all costs. Only by acknowledging our reality—even the painful parts—can we journey to wholeness.

Here are three questions we can ask ourselves that can open the door to discovering who we are in God:

1. What are the virtues and qualities that brought me to where I am now—in my faith and beliefs, my work, my relationships, my state of life?

2. What are those things that contribute to or take away from my potential for wholeness?

3. What is that true self in me trying to emerge? What kind of person do I wish to grow into? What are those virtues I wish to foster or continue fostering?

Jesus said not to hide a light under a basket. Our true identities (which for me includes my Eightness) mustn't be hidden from the world. God instills within us a unique character that's yearning to shine out in the open. We must claim our reality, our stories, and our identities to be whole people who are called to make a *unique* contribution to God's plan for the world. Our identities are bound up in the unfolding of God's creation.

FREEDOM AND DETACHMENT

Our truest selves live in a spirit of detachment. Imagine that you get handed a check for $100,000. It's from an anonymous source, but it's gifted to you, and there are no conditions attached to it. You can do whatever you want with it. So what do you do?

Here's the thing: you're a follower of God. You're a good person, you pray, you only look to deepen your relationship with God—and you don't want anything, even money, to stand in the way of that. This sum of money given to you presents a challenge for you. Do you spend it? How? Do you give it away, or do you hold on to it? The bottom line is that this money can easily become an attachment that will distract you in your spiritual life.

"Do not store up treasure on earth," the scriptures say. But what's so bad about material things? In short, nothing. All the created world was made for good, as is confirmed in Jesus' incarnation. So what would you do with a lot of money?

St. Ignatius presents this very problem in the Spiritual Exercises under a meditation known as "Three Classes of People."[5] He presents three different reactions to the situation I just described:

- The first type of person wants to rid himself of the money so he can focus on God. He knows it would be the right thing to not have such an attachment looming over him, but, for one reason or another, he never takes action.

- The second kind of person bargains with God. She knows it's best to get rid of the money, but she's just too attached to it, so she says, "I'll give $1,000 to charity and a little money to my neighbor," and she tries to convince herself that that is good enough. She wants things on her own terms and is still clearly attached to the money.

- The third type wants no attachment to the money, but for him it's not about keeping it or not keeping it. He simply wants what God wants. This person is truly free. He's not attached to the money but rather wishes to discern God's will for it.

In the "Principle and Foundation" section at the beginning of the Spiritual Exercises, St. Ignatius says that we are created to praise, reverence, and serve God and that all material things are created to help us to this end. And we must use material things (such as money) insomuch as they help us in glorifying God and rid ourselves of material things if they prevent us from glorifying God.[6] This is the kind of freedom the third kind of person in the meditation came to have.

Much focus has been placed on Pope Francis and his simplicity and lived material poverty, his doing away with certain opulence and papal "perks." But for the pope, who is a Jesuit and who has prayed with this very meditation about material things, it's about an indifference to such things. This Ignatian indifference means he neither wants these material things nor doesn't want them, but rather he wants what is beneficial in his ministry of building up God's kingdom. The focus is shifted from the self to God. Certain attire may indeed be of benefit to the pope's ministry. Flying in a plane or driving in a car helps the end of spreading the Gospel message far and wide. But what ultimately leads the pope in his use of material things is his discernment of God's will. Once free from attachment, a material thing can be used or disposed of according to what best serves one's life purpose of serving God and bringing God's love to the world. And this is true wholeness: freedom and detachment from the things that hold us back from being the person God made us to be.

I spent some time ministering in Kingston, Jamaica, to an impoverished community of people. Many of the children I met in the school had no fathers in their lives. They were often kept up at night in fear by the sounds of gunfire between police and drug lords. Families lived in run-down apartments or shacks next to open sewers. They didn't have much in the sense of material goods. But when I met the people in the "yards," as they call them, or when I saw them in church, I saw tremendous joy in them. They wore their one and only Sunday outfit each week and went to church praising God for the blessings in their lives. They gave thanks for God's goodness.

These people were broken in many ways, as we all are, but their wholeness shone through in their detachment from material things. Sure, their detachment wasn't by choice, but they didn't cling to what they didn't have, like many so often do. They had true freedom, and they weren't held back from praising, reverencing, and serving God. I witnessed the kind of freedom and detachment Jesus witnessed in his day. The Gospel of Mark tells the story of an old widow who put in the Temple collection box two coins—all she owned. There were rich people who put in what they could spare, such as the second type of person in Ignatius's meditation, because they were still clinging to their riches. But the widow, Jesus told his friends, "poor as she is, put in all she had—she gave all she had to live on" (Mk 12:44a, GNT).

It's not just material things that we're called to be detached from. We're called to let go of status and power. It doesn't matter whether you're a CEO, a priest, a teacher, or unemployed and living on the street. We're all susceptible to grasping for power, regardless of our situations. Even Jesus, to whom we give the title the "God-man," humbled himself. As St. Paul said, Jesus "did not regard equality with God something to be grasped." Instead, he "emptied himself," became a servant, and chose to be poor (Phil

2:6–8, NABRE). There were no unfreedoms holding Jesus back from serving his Father. Even his miracles were not for showing off but for revealing God to his followers.

Jesus reveals the fullness of being human through humility all the way to the Cross. David Fleming says, "Humility lies in the acceptance of Jesus Christ as the fullness of what it means to be human."[7]

In the Spiritual Exercises, St. Ignatius offers some notes on three degrees of humility or, as I would call them, three degrees of wholeness.[8] The first degree is doing what's absolutely necessary in our lives to follow God's commandments. In this degree, we may keep our possessions and current ways of life, but we do everything we can to avoid sin and to be Christlike.

The second degree comes with a desire to free ourselves from the things that hold us back, such as giving in to our "core sins" and other tendencies. We may rid ourselves of certain things so we can follow God even more closely.

The third degree comes with a complete desire to be like Christ, poor rather than rich and completely accepting the suffering that comes from weakness. It's complete detachment from material things and from comforts in order to be more whole God-followers.

To genuinely praise, reverence, and serve God—the reason we were created—we must be in a state of freedom. The weaknesses that are often a part of who we are don't hold us back from this freedom; sin and unhealthy attachments to status, power, and things do.

I don't believe Ignatius would say that having a large house, owning an iPad, or being a business executive are *bad*. They're certainly not inherently evil. But Ignatius is calling us not to *cling* to those things. He calls this "indifference." Almost nonchalantly, one would say, "[I] feel no inclination to have riches rather than poverty, to want honor rather than dishonor, to desire a long life rather than a short life."[9] And just like with that surprise $100,000 check, a person with true indifference is inclined neither to hold on to it nor to give it away. Instead, this person is motivated to determine how this *thing* (or position of power, or iPad, or car) can be used to serve God and bring God into the world in some way. Or perhaps one could ask, "Can this thing give God skin?"

Ignatius also calls us not to cling to certain plans or agendas in our lives. These things can hold us back not only from happiness but also from being open to God's blessings. When I was on that eight-day silent retreat, I was preparing to start a master's program in theology and wanted the retreat to be a time to focus on that transition to studies. I had also just recently gotten engaged and wanted to pray about that, too. I also brought a few spiritual books I had been wanting to read. Needless to say, I had lots of plans for what God was supposed to do for me on retreat. What happened, as often happens on retreat, was that my plans went out the window! Instead, my retreat became all about freedom. God was calling me to let go of my plans and agendas for the week and instead rest in God's presence.

I was initially like the Samaritan woman at the well. Jesus had other plans for her, but she was caught up with her agenda of fetching a bucket of water. Jesus wanted to give her "living water," new life, yet she continued to focus on retrieving actual water from the well. "Sir, give me this water, so that I may not be thirsty or have to keep coming here to draw water" (Jn 4:15, NABRE). The woman missed the point. She was not letting go of her own plans, even though Christ was in front of her.

My spiritual director caught on to the trajectory my retreat was taking (where the Spirit was moving me) and one day suggested I go to the retreat center art room and draw a mandala. A mandala is a circular drawing that can aid in letting go of our preconceived plans. I began in the center of a sheet of paper and began drawing outward with colored pencils. The color I chose would be the color that first came to mind. The shape I'd draw would be the first one to arise from within. Instead of planning what the mandala would look like, I let the Spirit lead the drawing. What resulted was a piece of artwork that came from a place of freedom, not planning.

I had many other experiences on the retreat of letting go of agendas. Not once did I pray about my life transitions. I did not read all the books I brought. God had other plans for my retreat!

Retreatants, faced by several days of silence and an absence of structure and schedules, often struggle trying to figure out what to do. They want peace and quiet, but their minds are distracted with other thoughts. Some are hoping to use the time to discern a big decision but find they can't seem to hear the voice of God. I once asked a man how he dealt with the unstructured time on a silent retreat. He told me that he would just sit in the chair of his room. "And what would you do?" I asked. He responded, "I had no plans. I might listen to music or sit there and pray. And if thoughts came to mind, I'd just ponder them. And if I fell asleep, then I fell sleep." That is true freedom and detachment!

ALLOWING LOVE

One of our greatest fears as human beings is not being loved. Reaching true human wholeness requires us to allow ourselves to be loved. Henri Nouwen says that Jesus' "freedom was rooted in his spiritual awareness that he was the Beloved Child of God."[10] Like a parent, it is impossible for God to unlove any of God's children—this includes us! Indeed, in the Bible, the evangelist John says simply, "God is love" (1 Jn 4:8 NABRE). Nothing more needs to be said. For God not to love means God would cease to exist. So why can it be so difficult to know we are loved by our Creator? Because we don't know how to receive God's love.

In human relationships—and this is perpetuated by stereotypes of love on TV and in movies—when one person says, "I love you," the other is expected to respond, "I love you, too." This expectation has become a norm, and, oddly enough, the recipient of the first person's love doesn't fully acknowledge the gift given. Instead, he or she fulfills the cultural expectation and bounces back with, "I love you, too." That's why in movies (and in real life), when someone says I love you, the other, not having the same feelings, awkwardly may respond the same even though his or her feelings don't match. Or he or she may freak out.

Though it seems strange, the best response to someone telling you that he or she loves you is "Thank you." That response says, "Thank you! I receive this gift from you and cherish it!" Adding an "I love you" is fine, but first *receiving* the love is most important. Because Jesus, who is the image of human wholeness, accepted and received God's love, he was free from having to give in to the expectations of the world. In the desert, he did not have to succumb to the temptations of the evil spirit because he knew the freedom that comes from God's love.

One of the simplest prayers is this: "God, you love me." Just receive God's love. So often we express love to God but fail to truly receive it. Ignatius ends the Spiritual Exercises with a meditation called "The Contemplation to Attain Love."[11] In it we're called to contemplate four ways God loves us: God's gifts to us, God's self-giving, God's laboring for us, and God's unceasing giving and gifting. In other words, we are asked to contemplate the many ways God penetrates our everyday reality.

First, we ponder the ways God has gifted us with possessions, life, clothing, food, and so on. These gifts allow us to serve God and serve the world. So whether it's the gift of money, food, a particular talent, or even the gift of our sexuality, God has given these things to us freely with the hope we'll use them to share our love with one another. In this way, all things become *sacramental*. That is, the tangible and intangible gifts God has given us can be used to bless others and in turn serve God.

We must also consider the ways God gives of God's self with us. This is ultimately done through the person of Jesus. God chose to become incarnate in order to be with us, side by side, as an example of human wholeness. Just as a friend gives of herself or himself by spending time with us, listening to us, and laughing with us, God wishes to become a friend to us in these same ways. Ignatius also speaks about God's love in the ways God labors for us. Behind the scenes, often without our awareness, the sun rises and sets each day, our white blood cells fight off infection, our food grows from the earth, and all the processes of the universe continue moment to moment. God's love comes to us through the unfolding of creation. Despite our brokenness and past sin, God tirelessly cares for us.

For all the ways God loves us, Ignatius asks us to *receive it*. Then he has us contemplate on how this love from God is endless and unceasing. There is no end to God's gifting, self-giving, and laboring. Yet how often do we pause long enough to notice this? How long do we pause to notice the ways God is continually connecting to our material world and intimately involved in our lives? Ignatius knew that to be fully human, fully whole, we must accept the love of God. When we trust that love, despite our biggest weaknesses, we are freed from seeking to be people we're not meant to be. In fact, true wholeness means we *become* part of the divine gift, the whole, or, if you like, part of the wholeness of the Body of Christ. As the rays of the sun are part of its light source or the waves are part of the ocean, we become part of God. Paul Coutinho describes this beautifully: "At the end of the Spiritual Exercises, you and the Divine become one. Not only do you and God become one, but also everything is seen as a manifestation of the Divine. You look at a tree and see God and experience God. It is a manifestation of the Divine. It is the presence of the Divine that makes a tree a tree. It is a miracle."[12]

Ignatius ends the meditation with his famous *Suscipe* prayer, a statement of faith that we can let go of (be indifferent to or detached from) everything we possess because God's love and grace are all we need.

Psalm 139 says, "I praise you, for I am fearfully and won-derfully made" (Ps 139:14a, NRSV). Just as Jesus was formed so intentionally by God in Mary's womb, created for a unique purpose, we too were made with care and intention, not to be someone else but to be our true selves: whole, free, and loved. Just as children are the product of their parents' love, we are the product of the divine love Ignatius has us immerse ourselves in. We might as well have a tag on us that says, "Made with Love"!

God brought us into the world, not to be St. Teresa of Calcutta or Bl. Óscar Romero or even Jesus but to be *ourselves*. Wholeness is accepting that. Wholeness is accepting the loved creation we are and are becoming.

A PATTERN OF SELF-REFLECTION

What began in his bed while Ignatius was recovering from his broken leg was a pattern of self-reflection. He had the luxury of time to reflect on his attachments, his unfreedoms, and his weak-nesses. As the years went on, Ignatius continued to learn how to let go of things, including religious scruples, that held him back from a life of wholeness and he slowly came to accept who God had made him to be. The self-reflection that began with his injury became a regular daily pattern of self-reflection in the form of his examen prayer. His journey to his true self has affected millions of people today who pray the examen every day.

Not only has the Ignatian examen moved so many to per-sonal growth, but the Spiritual Exercises's framework of asking for a grace and being attentive to the movements of the good and evil spirits has given us tools to grow into wholeness. Most importantly, scripture shows Jesus' continual pattern of pausing in prayer before returning to ministry. I imagine his prayer times let him tap into God's call for him to continue to be fully human, fully whole. He wore no masks and never tried to be someone else. Yet for some reason, we have a hard time taking off our own masks. We are sometimes unaware that we're even wearing them, hiding God's fullness from the world. Anthony de Mello, a Jesuit mystic, often provocatively said that most of us are asleep. We go about this world unconscious and unaware. He calls us to wake up and look at ourselves! It took a cannonball to the leg to wake up Ignatius. Thankfully, we can be awoken not by an injury but by the stories of those around us whose false selves and attachments have brought little joy or wholeness. We can look at celebrities, politicians, and those in the news who are not in a pattern of honest self-reflection but in a pattern of sorrow and addiction and desire for power. Jesus was awake because he sought none of those things. Humility and freedom were his pattern. Making self-reflection and prayer a daily pattern can move us toward the human beings God wants us to be. If our responsibility as Christians is to help make God manifest in a broken world then it is also our responsibility to seek our own healing and wholeness.

CONCLUSION

We only have to look up, and God's there, gazing upon us. It's that magic C. S. Lewis talks about, that invisible divine power made visible in the created world, in the things we can see, and in the little ordinary miracles of everyday life. But mysteriously, God also dwells in the broken and messy parts of our lives, looking to make whole again the pieces. There is no place that God is not lurking, seeking us out, and being revealed.

That an infinite God became human is the center of the Christian faith. It was a pinnacle moment in human history that changed everything. This is why the central encounter with the divine for Ignatius occurs in an encounter with a God who has skin. Ignatius has built a rich tradition of prayer that helps us tap into our real-life experiences and emotions as a way to discern God's activity. As Christians, our lives are held together by this incarnational nature.

Jesuit Karl Rahner once said, "Thanks to Your mercy, O Infinite God, I know something about You not only through concepts and words, but through experience. I have actually known You through living contact."[1] Ignatian spirituality helps expand God's palpable presence to all of creation, to our relationships, and to our interior feelings. So real is this presence that we believe God communicates *directly* to us through this created world—and

even through the stuff we've created. God can speak to me in an
encounter with a coworker, a blog post I read, a walk down an
urban street, and even music and art. When we recognize God
in the everyday, the narrow views we may have of prayer bloom
into a myriad of ways to encounter God. When this happens, it
doesn't matter how messy and broken our lives can feel; we're
able to encounter God no matter what or where or when.

Our human family seems to embody well a God who wishes
to be everywhere. We are people from all around the world, with
different backgrounds and gifts, and in countless fields of work.
Through our different gifts, we help make God present to people
all over the world. God is manifest through people like you and
me, who are called to share our unique gifts with others. And this
sharing comes about through our vocations.

Since God is intimately involved with our life choices, God
calls us to look within and without to discover what part we
have to play in God's project for the world. When God's dreams
come true in us, we actually bring God more into the world. And
Jesus is the one we can look to for a pattern of discovery, since he
himself represents the human ideal of wholeness—which even
includes weakness and mistakes. Our friendship with the Word
made flesh opens us up to deep transformation. To paraphrase
a poem attributed to Pedro Arrupe, our relationship with God
will affect all we do: the people we meet, the choices we make,
and the ways we find joy. An encounter with God in the person
of Jesus transforms the way we live our lives.

A universal encounter with God seems to be the theme
Pope Francis has been taking in his papacy. In fact, a Dominican
priest believes that the pope has been quietly leading the Church
through the Spiritual Exercises.[2] As one who has made the Exercises at least twice, the pope is calling all of us to what he calls "a
culture of encounter"—with one another, but most importantly
with Jesus. His homilies and addresses often reference the imagination, the good and evil spirits, colloquy, discernment, and

other Ignatian themes. He is reminding us that we have a God who cares for us *intimately*.

It's hard for many to imagine such a personal God. The God of my childhood who lived up in the clouds was shattered when I discovered that God can be found in all things. The world around me took on so much meaning. The material world, as Ignatius states so clearly, was created for glorifying God. Even the decisions I made seemed to have a greater purpose.

So consider now how all these previous pages have opened up to you. Consider this God we have, who infinitely and endlessly remains present, loving, and open for friendship and conversation. What does the Incarnation mean to you, that an infinite God took on human skin and asked us also to partake in his mission? We're not asked to do it all, but our contribution is critical. It happens in how we choose to use money, what we choose to read, those we choose to spend time with, where we choose to live, and how we choose to live our lives. Life is an endless string of little choices. But all those choices and decisions must be informed by our here-and-now encounter with the divine.

The Incarnation of Christ blurred the line between the sacred and profane. Dirty feet can be as holy as a chalice. A vocation in marketing can be as holy as a vocation to be a priest. There's no "higher" calling; we're called simply to be the one God made us to be. And that whole person we're called to be can truly be guided by the wisdom Ignatius gave to us: the rich framework of Ignatian spirituality. It's a spirituality that frees God from any boxes or boundaries we've created. It's a spirituality that offers a direct two-way connection with a God who so deeply loves us and cares about every little thing we do, who wants us to use our gifts for the transformation of the world.

The message of this book you hold is simply this: God can be found within human reality. While many of us may begin our spiritual lives looking for God *solely* in religious ritual, formulaic prayers, or scripture, we must move beyond that and see God *also* in our lived experiences.

There's a Sufi story that sums this up well:

> One night the poet Awhadi of Kerman was sitting on his porch, bent over a vessel. Shams e-Tabrizi happened to pass by.
> Shams: "What are you doing?"
> Awhadi: "Contemplating the moon in a bowl of water."
> Shams: "Unless you have broken your neck, why don't you look at the moon in the sky?"[3]

We need to redirect our gaze from a faded reflection of God to the *actual* God! The scribes and Pharisees of the gospel stories were still trying to look at a reflection of God—only what their laws and tradition told them (which were not bad in themselves)—rather than looking up and seeing God standing right before them in the person of Jesus. Our encounters with God occur when we look at *reality*. In the gospels, people only had to look up at Jesus and see God. In the Hebrew Scriptures, God was found in a pillar of cloud or in a burning bush or in a small whisper. In our present day, God can be found in the natural world; in our friends, in our families, and in the strangers around us; in our jobs; in the Church; in our prayers and reflection; and in our choices.

We call God the Alpha and the Omega, the beginning and the end, because of God's infinite embrace of all creation. As we move about each day, we are part of that infinite embrace. My spiritual director was right about God—I didn't need to go to any special place. I simply needed to open my eyes and look around, look within, and see that God takes on skin in every part of life.

ACKNOWLEDGMENTS

I first would like to thank my wife, Sarah, who has been my biggest supporter in this project. Sarah has not only read and edited my manuscript and influenced my theology but she also encourages and affirms me every day, reminding me that I am loved despite my imperfections. My parents, Alison and Jeff, who were the genesis of my faith journey, deserve heaps of gratitude for their continuous trust in my vocation as I discerned to enter and later leave religious life and then to get married. I'm especially grateful to my brother Brent, a Jesuit priest, who has always been an inspiration to my spiritual life. He is always advocating for me as an Ignatian lay minister in the Church. I love my family dearly.

As is clear in this book, I believe spiritual direction is crucial in our spiritual formation and discernment. I would like to thank all those I've had as spiritual directors over the last several years, including John Wronski, S.J., who, as my first spiritual director, taught me about Ignatian prayer, helping me discern to enter the Society of Jesus. Joe Costantino, S.J., helped me see the Spirit's movement in my dreams and desires as I was discerning to leave religious life. And John Predmore, S.J., met me on the other end as I adjusted back to life outside the Jesuits. John is a wonderful spiritual director and friend who companioned me in my discernment to marry Sarah. I'm grateful for these three men and everyone in between, including all those with whom I worked in my various apostolates and ministries throughout the years. Most of all, I'm grateful for Jesus, with whom St. Ignatius calls us to be friends. Both Jesus and Ignatius worked hard to surprise me with a life's journey I never imagined for myself!

NOTES

INTRODUCTION

1. Ronald Rolheiser, *The Holy Longing* (New York: Random House, 1999), 95.

1. AWARENESS

1. C. S. Lewis, *Letters to Malcom: Chiefly on Prayer* (San Diego: Harcourt, 1992), 103–104.

2. The Michael Gungor Band, "Cannot Keep You," in *Beautiful Things* (Brash Music, 2010).

3. Holly Bird, "Five Beauty Tips," *God in All Things* (blog), January 9, 2015, accessed January 23, 2015, https://godinallthings.com/2015/01/09/five-beauty-tips-for-2015.

4. Richard Rohr, "Religionless Christianity," *Richard Rohr's Daily Meditation* (blog), May 24, 2015, http://conta.cc/1HklGcL.

5. John of Damascus, quoted in "St. John of Damascus: On the Holy Images," *Orthodox America*, accessed November 22, 2014, http://www.roca.org/OA/95/95b.htm.

6. Rolheiser, *The Holy Longing*, 77.

7. Ibid., 78.

8. *Catechism of the Catholic Church*, 460, Vatican website, accessed July 13, 2015, http://www.vatican.va/archive/ccc_css/archive/catechism/p122a3p1.htm.

9. Bernadette Farrell, "O God, You Search Me," in *Christ Be Our Light* (OCP, 1994).

10. Joseph Tylenda, S.J., ed., *A Pilgrim's Journey: The Autobiography of Ignatius of Loyola*, rev. ed. (San Francisco: Ignatius Press, 2001), 78–79.

11. Ignatius of Loyola, *Spiritual Exercises* (Charlotte, NC: TAN Books, 1996), annotation 315.

2. PRAYER AND SPIRITUAL PRACTICES

1. Francis, *Evangelii Gaudium*, sec. 90, Vatican website, accessed July 13, 2015, http://w2.vatican.va/content/francesco/en/apost_exhortations/documents/papa-francesco_esortazione-ap_20131124_evangelii-gaudium.html.

2. William A. Barry, S.J., and William J. Connolly, S.J., *The Practice of Spiritual Direction* (New York: HarperOne, 2009), 23.

3. Ignatius of Loyola, *Spiritual Exercises*, annotation 75.

4. Margaret Bullitt-Jonas, *Holy Hunger: A Woman's Journey from Food Addiction to Spiritual Fulfillment* (New York: Vintage Books, 2000), 107.

5. Rachel Naomi Remen, *My Grandfather's Blessings: Stories of Strength, Refuge, and Belonging* (London: Penguin Books, 2000), 216–217.

3. DISCERNMENT

1. Dave Prafitt, "Interview with Walt Disney Imagineering Legend Marty Sklar on Creating Magic Kingdoms," *Adventures by Daddy*, July 12, 2013, accessed January 29, 2015, http://www.adevnturesbydaddy.com/2013/07/12/interview-with-disney-imagineering-legend-marty-sklar.

2. George Aschenbrenner, S.J., *Stretched for Greater Glory: What to Expect from the Spiritual Exercises*. (Chicago: Loyola Press, 2004), 8.

3. Paul Coutinho, S.J., *An Ignatian Pathway* (Chicago: Loyola Press, 2011), 19.

4. "Adolfo Nicolás: The Strength of Ignatian Spirituality," YouTube video, 1:27, from a speech given in Belgium on September 26, 2010, accessed January 29, 2015, https://www.youtube.com/watch?v=bGhcI3zhnjQ.

5. Louis M. Savary, *The New Spiritual Exercises* (New York: Paulist Press, 2010), 87.

4. WHOLENESS

1. David Brooks, *The Road to Character* (New York: Random House, 2015).

2. Ignatius of Loyola, *Spiritual Exercises*, annotation 58.

3. Ibid., annotation 60.

4. Savary, *The New Spiritual Exercises*, 47–48.

5. St. Ignatius of Loyola, *Spiritual Exercises*, annotation 149ff.

6. Ibid., 23.

7. David L. Fleming, S.J., *Draw Me Into Your Friendship: A Literal Translation and Contemporary Reading of the Spiritual Exercises* (St. Louis, MO: Institute of Jesuit Sources, 1996), 129.

8. Ignatius of Loyola, *Spiritual Exercises*, annotation 165ff.

9. Fleming, *Draw Me Into Your Friendship*, 128.

10. Henri J. M. Nouwen, *Bread for the Journey: A Daybook of Wisdom and Faith* (New York: HarperOne, 1997), May 20.

11. Ignatius of Loyola, *Spiritual Exercises*, annotation 230ff.

12. Paul Coutinho, S.J., *How Big Is Your God? The Freedom to Experience the Divine* (Chicago: Loyola Press, 2007), 65.

CONCLUSION

1. Karl Rahner, S.J., quoted in Jim Campbell, "Karl Rahner, SJ (1904–1984)," *Ignatian Spirituality*, accessed February 6, 2016, http://www.ignatianspirituality.com/ignatian-voices/20th-century-ignatian-voices/karl-rahner-sj.

2. Cindy Wooden, "Theologian Sees Ignatian Approach in Pope's Reflections for Synod," *The Pilot*, June 1, 2015, accessed July 13, 2015, http://www.thebostonpilot.com/article.asp?ID=173946.

3. Massud Farzan, "Moon in a Bowl of Water," Spiritual-Short-Stories.com, accessed May 30, 2015, http://www.spiritual-short-stories.com/spiritual-short-story-470-Moon+In+A+Bowl+of+Water.html.

ANDY OTTO is a Catholic writer, speaker, blogger, spiritual director, and podcaster who teaches theology and is the campus minister at Mercy High School in Red Bluff, California.

Otto earned a degree in communications from Curry College in 2006 and spent almost three years as a Jesuit seminarian before discerning marriage. He earned a master's degree in theology and ministry from the School of Theology and Ministry at Boston College in 2015.

Otto created and edits *God in All Things*, and he also founded the website *Ignatian Resources*. He previously worked as programming and acquisitions coordinator at CatholicTV. He has contributed to *Busted Halo*, *America* magazine, *Millennial* journal, and *Ecojesuit*. Otto and his wife, Sarah, live in Chico, California.

AVE MARIA PRESS

Founded in 1865, Ave Maria Press,
a ministry of the Congregation of
Holy Cross, is a Catholic publishing
company that serves the spiritual and
formative needs of the Church and its
schools, institutions, and ministers;
Christian individuals and families; and
others seeking spiritual nourishment.

For a complete listing of titles from

Ave Maria Press

Sorin Books

Forest of Peace

Christian Classics

visit www.avemariapress.com

AVE MARIA PRESS
Notre Dame, IN
A Ministry of the United States Province of Holy Cross